W9-ARL-851

SEEKING FREEDOM

Bishop Samuel Ruiz
In conversation with
Jorge S. Santiago

On time and history, prophecy, faith and politics, and peace

Translation from the Spanish and editing by
Michel Andraos

**Toronto Council of the Canadian Catholic Organization for
Development and Peace**

Original title in Spanish: *La búsqueda de la libertad, Entrevista realizada en septiembre de 1996 a Mons. Samuel Ruiz García por Jorge Santiago Santiago*

Editors of the Spanish edition: Jorge Santiago and Ana de Saint Phalle

Copyright © 1999, San Cristóbal de Las Casas, Chiapas, Mexico.

English edition copyright © 1999 by Michel Andraos. All rights reserved.

Printed in Canada

Cover photo: Siobhan Rowan
Photo art work: Gaby Andraos
Cover design and layout: Michel Andraos

Distribution:

Toronto Council - Development and Peace
10 St. Mary Street, Suite 420
Toronto, Ontario M4Y 1P9
Canada
Tel. 416/922-1592, ex. 25
Email: srowan@devp.org

ISBN: 0-9683714-6-9

*In honour of Bishop Samuel Ruiz,
the Indigenous communities of Chiapas
and their struggle
for a life with peace, justice, and dignity*

CONTENTS

FORWARD

Our solidarity links with Bishop Samuel Ruiz and the diocese of San Cristóbal de Las Casas go back more than two decades. The work of Don Samuel and the diocese of San Cristóbal have been a great sign of hope to our world.

We present *Seeking Freedom* to our members and to all those who are involved in social justice work. We hope this brief presentation of Don Samuel's thought, vision and spirituality will strengthen our faith and deepen our commitment to work for a more just world.

Our work in solidarity with the people of Chiapas in their struggle for peace, justice and dignity has greatly enriched us. So too have our trips to the diocese of San Cristóbal over the last few years. The testimony of the visitors we have received from Chiapas has been powerful and inspirational. We feel a deep solidarity with the suffering yet hopeful people of Chiapas, their Church, and their social movements. This publication is one more step on our journey of solidarity.

In appreciation of Bishop Ruiz's life long commitment to the Church of the poor and to the Indigenous communities of Chiapas, the Toronto Council of Development and Peace is honoured to present *Seeking Freedom*, the English edition of *La Búsqueda de la Libertad*.

Many people have suffered and died in Chiapas. We remember them all. May their vision of a more humane world, where peace and justice prevail, continue to inspire us.

Toronto Diocesan Council
Development and Peace

PREFACE

Bishop Samuel Ruiz, or *Tatic Samuel*,* as the Native peoples of Chiapas call him, turned 75 on November 3, 1999. He has submitted his resignation as bishop of the diocese of San Cristóbal and is waiting for its acceptance by the Vatican and the nomination of a new bishop to replace him. But the place he has occupied in the heart of the Indigenous communities of Chiapas, the faithful of his diocese and the many people from around the world who visited Chiapas and had the chance to meet him will be very difficult to fill. He has been a very special bishop with a particular gift of the Spirit. In carrying out his prophetic ministry, Don Samuel has been a voice that demands justice for the Native and poor campesinos of his diocese and identifies the causes of their poverty and oppression. He has unmasked the "social sin" of our society at this moment in history and become a universal voice heard far beyond Chiapas.

On a personal note, spending the last five years studying the theology of Bishop Ruiz and the pastoral process of the diocese of San Cristóbal as part of the research for my doctoral dissertation has been a very rewarding experience. Don Samuel's theology--which in many ways is the expression of the diocesan process--opens new avenues for theological reflection on some universally significant issues such as faith and politics, Church and cultures, human rights, mediation, peacemaking and reconciliation. *Seeking Freedom* is a small window through which we can have a glimpse of the life and work of a man of faith, vision, hope, and unwavering commitment to the cause of justice for the poor in his diocese and beyond.

This book is an edited translation of the manuscript of an interview conducted by Jorge S. Santiago in September of 1996. An edited Spanish version of this interview, *La Búsqueda de la Libertad*,

---

Tatic is a term of endearment that Native communities gave to Bishop Ruiz. It carries the meaning of 'father,' 'teacher' and 'elder' in some of the Native Mayan languages of Chiapas.

has just been published in San Cristóbal. The two appendices are also edited transcripts of more recent interviews which were conducted in the presence of the translator and editor of this edition.

This publication is the fruit of a collaborative effort of the Chiapas Working Group of the Toronto Council of Development and Peace. But, all errors in translating the thought of Bishop Ruiz and his interviewer are my responsibility. It is not an easy task to capture and communicate an interview in a written text. We trust that we have been as faithful as possible to the original manuscript.

I would particularly like to thank the members of the Chiapas Working Group for their dedicated efforts to promote solidarity with the people of Chiapas. Working together on various educational and solidarity projects has been a pleasure and a great learning experience. Special thanks go to Keith Gauntlett, Steve Taylor and Siobhan Rowan for their help with the proofreading and editing of the manuscript. Many thanks also to the Congregation of Notre Dame for their grant which helped us with this publication.

Michel Andraos
Toronto, November, 1999

INTRODUCTION*

Samuel Ruiz García has been bishop of the diocese of San Cristóbal de Las Casas in Chiapas, Mexico since January 25, 1960. He was the first bishop to be consecrated in the Cathedral of San Cristóbal since the creation of the diocese by Pope Paul III on March 19, 1539.

On November 3, 1996, Don Samuel turned 72. According to Church law, he has to resign from his position as bishop of the diocese when he turns 75. Only three more years left for him to walk the mountains of Chiapas preaching his universal vision.

A lot has happened during his time here! It has been a long life of great depth and openness to the future, transcending the present with its intensity.

In the State of Chiapas in southeastern Mexico, at the border with Guatemala, many significant social transformations have taken place in the last forty years.

It is important to identify some characteristics and points of reference in this time so that we can better understand the reflections that Don Samuel articulated in this interview of September, 1996.

One of these points of reference is the composition of the Indigenous peoples of Chiapas: Tzotziles, Tzeltals, Lacondones, Tojolabales, Cakchiqueles, Zoques, Cho'les and Mames. These Indigenous peoples have been recovering and strengthening their identities through a new awareness-raising and an on-going effort to return to their ethnic and cultural roots. By so doing, they have managed to resist and survive the battles of integration and cultural annihilation caused by the dominant Western culture.

At the Indigenous Congress in San Cristóbal in October of 1974, representatives of the Indigenous communities gathered to address the issues of land, trade, health and education. They sketched

---

*This introduction was written by Jorge Santiago in December of 1996, shortly after he conducted the interview.

1

out a program of action which, with time, was transformed into a struggle for dignity, autonomy and self-determination, and which demanded the participation of the Mexican Indigenous peoples (56 different ethnic groups in total) within the nation.

At the end of the 1996 National Indigenous Congress, Native representatives from all over Mexico asserted the above mentioned claims and demanded:

> First: legal and constitutional recognition of our existence as peoples and of our inalienable right to self-determination as articulated in the definition of the Mexican state.

> Second: constitutional recognition of our ancestral territories and lands which form the totality of our habitat where we maintain our physical and spiritual existence as peoples.

> Third: recognition of our normative Indigenous juridical traditions in the building of a pluralist judicial system which incorporates the various concepts and practices of justice which are used for maintaining order in Mexican society.

> Fourth: recognition of our differences and our capacity for self-government which integrates our own visions of autonomy and democracy, practiced as the power of the people.

> Fifth: recognition of all our social, political and cultural rights and the affirmation of the growth and continuity of our communities and peoples.

In the early seventies, after a symposium on "Inter-ethnic Relations in South America" (Barbados, January, 1971), governments, churches and anthropologists began to reflect on their responsibility towards the situation of the Indigenous peoples. Anthropologists thought that they knew about Native peoples; they were the specialists who were in a position to defend the right to existence of Native communities against colonization by dominant cultures and systems-- including the missions of the churches.

The vision expressed above began to change gradually with the rise of land claims and political struggles and movements of the peoples of Latin America. This included many Native peoples. Now the Indigenous peoples of the continent are the subjects of their own struggles and history. There is a light which continues to shine with every new day among Native peoples. The declaration "Never again a Mexico without us" of the National Indigenous Congress held from October 8 to 12, 1996, in Mexico City also marked a new dawn. 1500 delegates representing the various Indigenous peoples of Mexico were present at the Congress. What they said there was an articulation of their vision emerging from their history and roots. The change from the position of the anthropologists at the Barbados symposium to the statement of the Native representatives at the National Indigenous Congress in Mexico City is very impressive.

It was during this time span that the alert conscience of Don Samuel was formed and became like the sure steps of the people he accompanied.

Another significant characteristic of the situation in Chiapas is social injustice. Native peoples have been violated in the confrontation with the dominant model, the world of the white and mestizo people. They try to assert themselves as a society while constantly being faced with racial discrimination which denies them their rights and dignity. This confrontation has significant consequences: unjust imprisonment, assassination, rape, subjugation to merciless exploitation with threats to remain silent in the face of all these injustices.

But the struggle for land remains the central issue. This struggle has gone on since the Spanish conquest. In recent years, there has not been one day without a land conflict caused by the structure of land ownership, delays in the application of agrarian laws, the power of big landowners, the corruption of the agrarian authorities and the pressure generated by constant population growth and an increasing demand for land. The struggle for land continues to be the fundamental one. In the worldview of Indigenous peoples, land is necessary for their survival as a people. Their struggle for Mother Earth cannot be resolved with solutions that focus only on economic productivity.

As a consequence of the struggle against the power of the state and the interests of large landowners and other economic powers, both national and foreign, another very serious element comes into play: repression.

The discovery of the Word of God in the course of struggle of these communities has generated a strong faith. The divine revelation and mystery has been manifested among them in manifold ways and made them a living gospel.

Along with this came the discovery of the possibility of becoming a church together; a mystical body with diverse charisms and services, participatory and active, prophetic and responsible, a faithful witness to their history and to death and resurrection. How many times have death and resurrection been celebrated and how many tears have been shed by these people? And how many pardons and reconciliations have taken place? All this has made their life a spring of living waters.

On the 1st of January 1994 the Zapatista National Liberation Army (EZLN) appeared before the world and declared war against the Mexican Army. Their First Declaration from the Lacandona Jungle, "Today We Say Enough is Enough!" points to the origins of the EZLN:

TO THE PEOPLE OF MEXICO:
MEXICAN BROTHERS AND SISTERS
We are a product of 500 years of struggle: first against slavery, then during the War of Independence against Spain led by insurgents, then to avoid being absorbed by North American

4

imperialism, then to promulgate our constitution and expel the French empire from our soil, and later the dictatorship of Porfirio Diaz denied us the just application of the Reform laws and the people rebelled and leaders like Villa and Zapata emerged, poor men just like us. We have been denied the most elemental preparation so they can use us as cannon fodder and pillage the wealth of our country. They don't care that we have nothing, absolutely nothing, not even a roof over our heads, no land, no work, no health care, no food nor education. Nor are we able to freely and democratically elect our political representatives, nor is there independence from foreigners, nor is there peace nor justice for ourselves and our children.*

Significant events have taken place since then. After 11 days of fighting, on January 12, 1994, Carlos Salinas de Gortari, president of Mexico, in his capacity as Supreme Commander of the Federal Army, declared a cease-fire. That same day, the Indigenous Revolutionary Clandestine Committee-General Command of the EZLN accepted the cease-fire. They saw it as a first step towards initiating a dialogue between the opposing parties. The EZLN ordered their troops to cease all military operations against the federal army and the positions they occupied.

From that moment on, Don Samuel has been involved in the mediation of this conflict. The role of mediation for him is not new: for most of his ministry he has acted as a mediator on behalf of the Indigenous and campesino communities in their conflicts with government authorities and the powerful. Since the emergence of the EZLN, his role as mediator has expanded and become the focus of his pastoral efforts. Don Samuel is like a spring of hope for a peace with justice and dignity which never stops flowing.

The task of mediation would not have been possible without an openness to dialogue, collaboration and the capacity to approach others. Profound links of solidarity have existed between the diocese

---

*EZLN homepage <www.ezln.org>

and other entities since the early years of his ministry. Don Samuel's vision includes not only the peoples of Latin America, but also those of many other parts of the world. His yearning for solidarity knows no limits. He has lately become an important participant in the World Council of Peace. His global vision allows him to see new historic possibilities for reaching peace in Chiapas, and it opens new avenues towards the new millennium--new like the new earth, and the new heaven.

After experiencing several important events with him, and spending many long days together searching for new alternatives, the opportunity to explore his thoughts has been very interesting work. I have discovered that the best way to get to the wellspring of his thought is to follow his path as a prophet who is connected to his time and history.

This interview is an intimate reflection. It is only the beginning of a testimony of the life and work of Bishop Samuel Ruiz García.

Here is the fruit of these months of work, and also the product of many shared years.

Jorge Santiago S.
Teopisca, Chiapas, Mexico
December of 1996

SEEKING FREEDOM

I - TIME AND HISTORY

Jorge Santiago Santiago: The intention of doing this interview, Don Samuel, is to reflect together on what could help open new avenues for building peace and to hear your thoughts and concerns on this subject. As an introduction to this reflection, could you share with us a little bit of your personal experience of time and history since you came to Chiapas?

Don Samuel: I would like to add to your question that personal experience would not have a lot of meaning and relevance unless it is recognized as the fruit of an experience which is not constructed by one person, but rather lived out collectively and evaluated in relation to an historic reference which is not of our own making. On the other hand, this experience can only make sense if it is seen in relation to service to the community. From this perspective, therefore, I believe that this interview will help me, as well as others, to reflect on how God's plan has been gradually unfolding in a concrete manner through the work that we have been doing, and how we gradually arrived at specific situations where the power of the Spirit was manifested to us.

The encounter with time and history here in Chiapas has been for me an interesting experience. Our immersion in the Indigenous reality of time and history--although we are not fully part of it--has greatly influenced me. People in the Indigenous communities live as if time belongs to them; time for them is less important than things that happen in time, which take priority over time. I am not totally immersed in this experience, however, my life has been influenced by it and by the way of life of these communities and their tranquil lifestyle.

I thought of this question about time when I first came to Chiapas. I went to visit my predecessor, Bishop Torre Blanca, who stayed here longer than all the other bishops who preceded him. I asked him how he had spent his 15 years here, and what advice he would give to me. I was thinking at that moment about these long years he had lived here and what they meant to him, and I wondered about the many years that would pass before I would have 15 years of pastoral experience in this place.

A few years later, I looked back one day and 17 years had already passed by--time here flew by very fast. Now, 36 years have passed, and if the many events that have happened were not there to serve as historic landmarks, it would feel like I had only come here yesterday. We did not have time for ourselves to reflect on what had been happening so that we could feel the time; what needed to be done next in the communities always moved us forward without us realizing it.

J. S. S.: What would be the most important stages in the journey of your pastoral work with the Indigenous communities?

Don Samuel: It is always a bit arbitrary to think of such work in terms of stages, and when we identify some, it is hard to say that they were the only ones. This also depends on where we are standing now and what we have as a historic reference.

If we think in terms of change in the way we do pastoral work, then we can name as one stage an event which had an impact on the whole continent, even on the whole world, namely the Second Vatican Council. This is a point of reference that marked our history as a diocese and also had an impact on all of Latin America; its repercussions were strongly felt at the meeting of the Latin American bishops in Medellín which took place shortly after the Council. It had a psychological and a theological impact on us who lived through all its stages, not only because of the consequences of the decisions that were made there, but it also affected us personally. It was a theologically educational event for us and a profound experience of transition. We learned at the Council what it means to build and become a Church. The Council also marked a step of maturity within the Church. We witnessed a very clear transition from a Church which announced a message as if given to it to apply to history, to a Church

9

that is looking through history to illuminate its message and see how the word of God becomes visible through historic events. This was a major transition and it clearly marked a new stage for us here in this diocese and elsewhere.

Another consequence of the Council was the critique of the pastoral work of the Church with Indigenous peoples which mainly came from the African bishops. This is reflected in the Council's document *Ad Gentes*, on the missionary work of the Church. The African bishops demanded that the Council discuss not only traditional missiology, but also new avenues and orientations to help find answers to the important questions which sociology, anthropology, and the social sciences in general, were asking the Church regarding its missionary work with Indigenous peoples. Also this reflection marked a new stage in our pastoral work and helped us bring it down to earth so that it responded to the specific situations of the people of our diocese. We were deeply affected by this questioning of the missionary activity and evangelization of the Church and how it should be transformed from a mere announcing of a message coming from outside to incarnating the gospel within cultures.

J. S. S.: What were some of the other important moments in the aftermath of the Council?

Don Samuel: We can mention here some of the events that took place outside of our diocese but which also had an impact on us and made us change our ways of doing things, without necessarily me personally being involved in them. Change for us in the beginning did not happen as a result of planned decisions made beforehand as to what should change and how to go about it. Change rather imposed itself on us as a demand of history. Obviously this occurred in a context of a thorough reflection on our history. After Vatican II, and especially after Medellín, the questions concerning our pastoral work with the Indigenous peoples became concrete. We began a long reflection in

10

which I participated very closely, first as a member of the Department of Missions of CELAM, and later as its coordinator. Through my work at CELAM, I was informed about all the theological activities which were taking place in Latin America after the Council in the area of evangelization and cultures. Here in Mexico, I was also on the Mexican Bishops' commission of Indigenous pastoral work. The team which was working on these issues, including CENAMI (El Centro Nacional de Ayuda a las Misiones Indígenas-The National Centre for Helping Indigenous Missions), took part in these new reflections and helped to implement them.

The proposed changes to the method of evangelization were part of a long term vision; they were the beginning of a process which continues to advance today. As a result of this process, some concrete steps were taken here in our diocese. One good example of this would be the 1974 Indigenous Congress which affected the whole diocese. This was a celebration or a commemoration of the life of Bartolomé de Las Casas and his passage through this diocese. An academic organization which bore his name came up with the idea of preparing an appropriate celebration for the occasion, and the organizers of the event asked us if we could collaborate with them. They were thinking of organizing conferences and inviting academics to give presentations on Bartolomé de Las Casas. We told them that we would collaborate with them and promote the project among the Indigenous communities and invite the people to come and listen to these important speakers, but we asked if it would not be better if we used this opportunity such that the Indigenous people could reflect on their situation and problems in light of the work and life of Las Casas. At that time, the various Indigenous groups were already working for their common cause, but each group was working on its own. We thought a meeting that would bring them together could provide an opportunity for them to collaborate.

Inviting the Indigenous communities to come together and listen to a series of speakers was not a bad idea. The organizers pointed out that in Michoacan, the Indigenous people knew who Tata

11

Vasco was; they talked about him, wrote poems about him, talked to tourists about his life as if he were with them, as if he were still alive and part of their contemporary history, while the Indigenous peoples of Chiapas did not know who Bartolomé de Las Casas was and they knew nothing about his work in defense of their rights. To me, the reason behind this is clear: Bartolomé only stayed here a total of less than six months. His physical presence did not leave many memories. The diocesan archives do not have any documents bearing his signature. Maybe some records which bear his name were kept somewhere else or were lost during the various movings of the archives, we do not know. However, it made sense to us to invite the communities of our diocese to come and listen to these people so that they might learn about Las Casas and his work.

The proposal was accepted, as you well know--you were present then and were part of the organizing team--and a brief biography of Bartolomé was prepared, translated into various Indigenous languages, and was distributed to the communities. Along with this an invitation was sent asking the people: "How does it appeal to you to participate in a reflection on your life situation today and what should be done to improve it in the context of a celebration of the life and work of Bartolomé de Las Casas?" This event was of great consequence for the diocese and that is why I regard it as a stage in our process. After the Congress four fundamental issues were identified as significant for the subsistence of the Indigenous communities: education, marketing of their products, etc. [land distribution, and health care]. In light of this analysis, we began to look at our diocesan pastoral plan which we were implementing and realized that it was up in the clouds; it did not have much to do with the real life problems of the people.

Hence, we had to revise our pastoral plan in light of these new points of reference that were brought to our attention at the Congress. We did not have back then the perception, which we only became aware of later, that a pastoral plan has to be based on the specific needs of the Indigenous people and not so much on the requirement to proclaim certain evangelical principles, which might or might not have an impact on people's real life and history. We did not realize then that the gospel is not a set of transcendent ideas, and that it could offer some answers to people's real problems and touch upon their daily lives. In this sense, the Indigenous Congress made us think of a down to earth pastoral plan which was more concrete, and which eventually led us to the long journey of working tenaciously in support of the emergence of the autochthonous churches in the diocese.

J. S. S.: I would like to ask you to also talk to us in this context about the option for the poor that was adopted at the diocesan assembly in 1975, shortly after the Indigenous Congress.

Don Samuel: Yes, this obviously was an important step which marked our process and was certainly related to the Indigenous Congress. We were concerned about the pastoral teams and their isolation in what they were doing. At the initial stage of their work, pastoral workers were spontaneously forming teams with other workers with whom they got along well. But the vast distances from one place to another and the geography of Chiapas are isolating. The Sierra Madre mountains are divided into two chains, eastern and western. They meet and form between them an immense territory which contains many hidden and isolated places. We began to think of how to elaborate an organic plan based on what was already happening so that we could develop and evaluate our work; if there were no clear objectives, goals, and means for us to evaluate our work, it would be difficult to know whether we were progressing or not, or in which direction we were going. Our work had immediate results and was effective, but we were not sure whether the long-term effects would be positive or negative.

We discovered at that moment that each and every one of our work plans was directed towards the poor, who formed the largest part of the population of our diocese and of whom the majority were

Indigenous. Without any intention of discriminating against the others, our work was spontaneously directed toward the areas where there was a greater need. Another factor that attracted us to these areas was that the results of our work among the poor were better. In some other areas we felt that our work was like a seed which fell on a land where the people trampled on it and it did not grow and give fruit. Therefore, it was more attractive for the missionaries and other workers who came to the diocese to go and work with the Indigenous communities--which also were more exotic because of their languages and mysterious world. But again, this was the area where the need was greater. That is how we realized, and without some prior agreement, that the poor got a preference in our pastoral action. We did not come to this agreement as a result of theological and philosophical debates; these were not the basis of our option. The process towards the making of this option was simple: the poor were there and we were working with them. The situation was such that if we had not worked with them there would have been nothing else for us to do. The poor were there and they became the centre of our concern. This decision was declared emphatically, but in a way it was simply an expression of what we already felt. It was not in any way a doctrinal imposition, it was a simple common reading of what we were already doing together. So, we agreed on this plan and said that no one had the right to sit idle in this diocese. We all had to be walking; some at the front, some in the middle and some at the back, according to the work we were doing, but no one had the right to be sitting or walking in another direction when we had all agreed that our action was going in this particular direction. Those among us who did not want this kind of work were given the choice to look for something else outside the diocese.

This is how we understood our option for the poor: a *de facto* practical option; the theological elaboration on this choice came later. When a broader theological explanation of the option for the poor became known, we in this diocese--although this might sound presumptuous--did not feel that we needed to root ourselves in it to be

14

able to move ahead in our work. The new theological explanation simply affirmed an option that was obvious for us: here are the people among whom God has chosen to put us to proclaim the gospel, we either work with them or we had better say that we do not want to follow the gospel or proclaim it. It was that simple. There was no need for a great theological treatise to explain this position.

There is another important moment which I hinted at earlier, before I talked about the Indigenous Congress, and which is also in a way related to the Congress. This moment was the specific reflection we did at a meeting of the pastoral workers convoked by CELAM which took place in Melgar, a small town in Colombia, to prepare for the bishops' conference in Medellín. It was there that the necessity to reflect on our pastoral action and how it was incarnated in the Indigenous cultures became clearer to us. In order to incarnate the gospel in these cultures, we needed to first understand God's presence among and revelation to the Indigenous peoples. When we greet the people during the liturgy in a language which is strange to them, and to us as well--but at least we have learned it, saying "Dominus vobiscum", "The Lord be with you," this is a sterile proclamation if we do not know in which manner God is present with these people. This is not a desire for God to be present with them, it is a proclamation and an affirmation of this presence. Therefore, we needed to learn in what way God is concretely present in their history, how is God present among them now, and what are the seeds of the Word which Vatican II mentioned--using the terminology of the Latin and Greek Fathers of the Church "*spermatu logu*" and "*semina verbi*"--to describe God's presence in other cultures. If we do not know them, how can we say that God is there? How can we build on this presence, not as a springing board, but rather to see how this manifestation of God has been happening among the Indigenous peoples and in other cultures. This was a significant conjuncture for us at national and continental levels.

After Melgar, a series of meetings were held in Mexico to discuss the concrete application of these reflections. One of these

meetings, which took place in Jicotepec, Juarez, was particularly
interesting. Among the participants present were Indigenous people
from Chiapas, some of whom are still with us today. There we
listened to the experience of the Indigenous peoples from across the
country and we also asked the Mexican anthropologists about their
point of view on Indigenous peoples' cultures. If we were going to
reflect on the incarnation of the Church among Indigenous cultures,
we needed to know first whether these cultures were still alive or
whether they were already dead or dying; if the latter was the case,
why then waste time determining how to incarnate the gospel in dead
cultures. Instead, we would prepare a nice epitaph for them.

We posed these questions to the anthropologists, since this is
their field. Curiously enough, and particularly so with the
anthropologists of the Mexican left, they did not only decline our
invitation, they totally rejected us and did not want any association
with us. Their image of us was that we were rigid dogmatists, not
capable of listening to and understanding what the social sciences
have to say, and above all they accused us of being professional
destroyers of cultures. It was a situation of terrible animosity.
However, Angel Palerma, a Catalan anthropologist who was at the
Iberoamerican university, knew about our discouragement and
advised us to wait a little bit and give it another try. He then came to
us saying, "Yes, they accept the invitation, but with one condition:
that you sit on the bench of the accused." This was the price to pay for
that invitation, but we accepted. The groups present took turns sitting
on the bench of the accused: first the National Indigenist Institute,
then the Catholics, and finally the Evangelicals--you probably
remember this because you were present there. We obtained good
results from these sessions. We met afterwards as bishops and then
with the Indigenous groups present who were in a parallel meeting
discussing the same issues. As a result of these meetings, the
anthropologists were impressed with our sincere attitude. We told
them how our relations had been with the Indigenous peoples before

and what the Council (Vatican II) is demanding of us, which also reflected our disposition and official position.

One of the anthropologists present, Arturo Bartman, congratulated us and we were invited to take anthropology courses, which a dozen people from our diocese--priests, religious and lay-- took over a period of three years. This was a new stage in our work where we began to understand a little bit about the Indigenous cultures and their background. The minimum that we were able to do then was to not impose on them our foreign language and instead to try to force ourselves to celebrate the liturgy in their languages. We then began the process of translating the scriptures and certain liturgical texts to their languages. And so began a new era in our diocese.

During an inter-diocesan meeting of the Southern Pacific region which took place in the county of Ocosingo, we discovered a new social reality. At the meeting were bishops from Guatemala and also the well known Canon Boulard. Based on the studies which were done in preparation for the meeting to help us understand and respond to our social situation, we came to the realization that, in contrast to the rest of Chiapas, Mexico and the Latin American continent, in the marginalized areas of Ocosingo, the rural population--not the urban population--was increasing. Many people were leaving their urban communities and moving into the jungle; rather than the other way around as was the trend in the rest of the continent. This phenomenon attracted our attention.

At the same time as we were searching for new ways to incarnate the gospel in Indigenous cultures, these communities in the jungle were also searching to understand their situation. They were not conscious of their past. When we asked them for dates and important personalities in their history, they did not know of any. They had the feasts of saints and the liturgical cycle with Christmas and the passion, death and resurrection of Christ--with more emphasis on the passion that on the resurrection. The question for us was, therefore, how can one found a Church which will be rooted in the

17

history of salvation of a community or a people who have no clear knowledge of their history. We had to make an effort to help them recover their more recent history. We simply asked them about the reason that lead them to leave their communities and migrate to the jungle, whether they wanted to go back or stay there and build their future, and how they were organizing themselves in the jungle. It appeared to us that the jungle was for them like a promised land. Migrating to the jungle was like a salvific call which lead them to leave the life of slavery, theft, exploitation and the lack of land. It was among them that the *Catechesis of the Exodus* emerged and through their Tzeltal pastoral team began to gradually spread to the rest of the diocese; it marked a new stage in the pastoral work of the whole diocese. A new method of catechism emerged: *tijuanej* replaced *snoptesjuanej*; that is, instead of the imposition of a doctrine, which was part of the old method, a new process emerged based on asking questions to stimulate participatory discussion. The method was passed on later in a natural way and became universal in the diocese. This was a new stage of change and growth which left its mark on our diocesan journey.

J. S. S.: These stages were not only local or personal, rather they were part of a broader and more universal movement. Do you feel that you were connected with the rest of the world in this process?

Don Samuel: No, we did not have an explicit perception of this. I think we came to this realization later. It was not a question of watching what were the new trends in the world and following them. Our process was imposed on us a result of the Indigenous world in which we lived. It became clear to us that evangelization as it had been happening had been a form of cultural oppression. Wherever the gospel was proclaimed to Indigenous people in the New World, with it came a new culture, namely the Western culture, and it was imposed on people as the only way of living the Christian faith. This imposition, therefore, created a real and visible cultural and religious schizophrenia with obvious symptoms among all the Native peoples in the continent. This was precisely the area to which we directed our pastoral attention. Obviously this was one of a gamut of other reflections that we were engaged in after the Council (Vatican II) which came to be known in Europe as the theology of temporal realities. That is, the Council recognized the independence of the temporal material world from the religious world, particularly in *Gaudium et Spes*, the document on the Church in the modern world. According to this document, the Council perceived creation to be autonomous, not subordinate to the religious but rather illuminated by it. All these ideas, therefore, were present and growing in the old world and they have influenced our post-conciliar debates and pastoral action with the Indigenous peoples--particularly with regard to the evangelization of cultures.

It became obvious to us that we are incarnating ourselves in the Indigenous cultures and we take into consideration the fact that God's presence among them predated our evangelization. This is a reality which we needed to recognize and come to grips with. To embrace this new attitude, we had to break away from the previous narrow historic vision and be open to accept the universal salvific presence of God in these cultures before our contact with them. We also realized that we were called to build on this presence and see our work as a continuity to the already existing salvific action of God in their history, adding to it our Christian faith experience. This is what we were encouraged to reflect on and do by the Council and that is what we began to do.

Since then, rather than do the same work of evangelization with both *mestizo* and Indian communities, and offer the same message to all without being aware of their different social classes, and ignore the fact that our work was not responding to the necessities of the Indian communities, we began to face our real world with all the conflicts in which these Indian communities live. We realized that their marginalization, poverty and misery were not the result of their free choice but rather were the result of a process in which we are

19

involved and which we need to rethink. When Christ said 'blessed are the poor,' it was not because they were destined to be poor for the rest of their lives, and not because they were going to always live in need, it is because the Reign of God was for them and because they were destined to inherit the land. It became obvious to us that what is meant here is not a symbolic, transcendent, post-historic reality. Rather, these affirmations imply a concrete historic realization as a part of the Reign of God here and now, and which will have its definite fulfillment in the time to come. In this sense, yes, we are part of a global reality and process. Our Church is not only focused on building itself from within, it also has a message to the outside world. This is clear to us.

J. S. S.: And what do you think is going to happen in the world?

Don Samuel: Aye! Don Pablo Gonzalez Casanova once gave me a crystal ball as a present so that I could look through it to see the future and be able to respond to such questions. It is hard to know what is going to happen. Generally speaking, we can say that there are certain coordinates and tendencies that show us the direction in which we are going. Based on this reading, some questions emerge concerning the future results of our work after all these years of collective and communal efforts--the pastoral work in the diocese is not mine, it is the work of many committed pastoral workers. There are areas where we see progress and where we can evaluate our work. Evangelization is not the only area where there is progress; it is part of a broader series of relations which influenced the Indigenous communities--of which we are only a part and by no means the only influence. We contributed to the process of transformation of these communities from being an object of the decisions of others to gradually becoming subjects of their own history. I believe this is the process we are in at the moment and it is irreversible: that is, the Indigenous peoples will continue to become subjects and this will perhaps lead to even more conflictive situations which would only make this process stronger;

this is what I mean by irreversible. The Indigenous and the poor have realized that they can influence history, that they are not only victims of history but are also able to transform the history which others have imposed on them, and that they have to not only resist the negative side of this history, but also to generate a new world for themselves and take responsibility for their concrete situation. I believe this is where the future is leading us. This is at the same time a path, a perspective, and an aspiration.

J. S. S.: Is the experience of becoming subject lived at the personal level?

Don Samuel: I believe so, although I did not think this was going to happen so soon. This does not mean that the Indigenous now stand and say to society, "Hey, look we are now subjects." But when they find themselves in certain situations where decisions need to be made, they say, "We now have to have our say, previously someone else spoke on our behalf." At the Indigenous Congress, if you remember, we had an extraordinary and unexpected answer from the Native participants when the pastoral workers asked them: "Who is Bartolomé de Las Casas for you now?" They almost unanimously replied: "It is us. We are Bartolomé. Once we needed someone to speak for us because we could not go to Spain to speak for ourselves. Now we can speak for ourselves." What we have now is the continuation of something that began then. It is not a question of making a decision: now we will stop being objects and become subjects. It is the result of the process of the new evangelization where the situation forced people not simply to wait for answers from others, but to actively search for their own answers. The Pope said to the Indigenous peoples in Yucatan: "You are the subjects of the evangelization of the continent. You, the Indigenous peoples, are the subjects of the transformation of the continent through peaceful, not violent means. Do not wait for others to act on your behalf; act yourselves and take on your historic responsibility. Become subjects

21

of history." I believe that this process has begun and it is an irreversible path. The Indigenous are living this reality, and we, who together with them are promoting this movement, are convinced that this should be our position inside the Church. We have a responsibility towards the Church. We are called to be reasonable, and not to proffer irrational obedience. This vision of transformation has a deep, divine foundation, and this is what gives us reason to take it up and promote it. As Paul wisely said, and he knew what he was talking about: to serve God is to reign. Becoming subjects of our history means reading God's plan and desire within historic events and, through these events, achieving the fullness of our potential of being human, and in this way reflecting the creation as a family and a community in communion with the divine family.

J. S. S.: What in your opinion would be some of the elements for building the future?

Don Samuel: The construction of the future has to be a common responsibility. For example, in building your house, no one should decide the way of construction more than you; that is, if you are going to have your own house and not live in a rented one. You ask for the services of an engineer or a builder, you choose according to your capacity, abundance or limitations the type of material you want and how much space you need. Others will help you in the technical aspects, but you are the one who is going to decide how you want your house built according to your needs. That is how all those who are owners and subjects build their homes. When we say this we are not talking only about the internal situation of our Church, or about the Reign of God which we build in a broader historic project. The question is how do the people today, the Indigenous of Chiapas and Latin America, want their home--which is everybody's home, but they as owners have to feel that they are inside the project--because they were living in this house before the others came; they should decide whether they want to renovate or re-build again from the foundations.

Therefore, in the building of the new house, the active word of each and every one of the present actors has to be considered in its historic articulation and concrete manifestations. Those who have taken ownership of the house and have hired others to work for them do not want there to be a change; they do not want to know that they are only the owners of a part of the house and cannot dominate the whole of it. The historic moment has arrived where each person is called to take their role and be in solidarity, co-responsible for the building of the Mexico we all want, the country we desire and also the Church we desire. This does not mean that the Church has to submit to our will, rather it has to respond to the expectations we hold, which are in accord with the will of God. We know that the Church is not democratic and decisions are not made according to the will of the people. Nevertheless, the Church provides certain principles and indications which guarantee the dignity of the human person. If we don't have this, as the psalm says, we will waste our time and build in vain; that is if the house is not built according to the will of the Lord, who saves us a lot of time by telling us, "Look, if you do not build this way, you will not be able to live in this house."

J. S. S.: What would be the approach necessary for people to become builders of the new house?

Don Samuel: Naturally there is a need to build the community dimension of living Christian charity. Charity is defending the other; it is the love of the other, this is what the scriptures teach us. Isaiah said: "Defend the right of others." Do not defend only your own right, defend the right of the other. The Bible says that we cannot find our own way if we are not searching for the way of the others as well. If we begin to work only for our own good and benefit, then we are on a path that destroys the possibility of building a house for the community. Therefore, the love of the other: which is at the heart of a disinterested endeavour; the patience and attentiveness for the opportune historic moment to advance; the effort needed for

23

understanding each other; the pedagogy for living together--these are all important dimensions for building together and they all derive from being in community, and are fundamental in this process. If there is something to be learned about living in community--and this is not only my experience, it is the experience of many others across the continent--it is from the Indigenous peoples that we can learn this because community is an essential dimension of their existence. Community life is a characteristic of the Indigenous from Alaska to Patagonia and this was not the fruit of an evangelization; it was something they had before the gospel. These are the seeds of the Word present in their cultures.

J. S. S.: To summarize this part: we feel we exist inside--and cannot live outside--time and history; this is a condition we need to accept.

Don Samuel: Correct. I believe that in this historicity lies precisely the conquest of the eternal--non-ephemeral--dimension of time. In the midst of this transition in time and history, there is an eternal dimension of living that goes beyond the minute which passes by. Eternity is at stake in every decision a person faces or makes at every moment in the relationship with one's community and history.

II - PROPHECY

J. S. S.: What does it mean for you to have faith at the present conjuncture in Chiapas and Mexico?

Don Samuel: I believe that faith sustains and illuminates our life. Without it, hope would have no foundation. Many ugly things have happened here in a short time: two or three years ago, I would never have believed that things such as burning people alive--not so much for reasons of personal vengeance, but because of a spread of collective outrage and violence resulting from the lack of justice-- could happen here if someone had told me. Like a big stain of oil that spreads quickly, the confusion caused by this deterioration was spreading across the country. This made other problems, such as narcotraficking, criminality, political deterioration and frustration, and inducement to violence, more rampant. In the midst of all this, if the Christian does not have a faith perspective, it makes it difficult to find meaning for life. For this reason, an insight illuminated by faith, as we have learned from our experience, does not come to us like an extraordinary light which appears suddenly and make us see and understand what is happening so that we find our way. Rather, this understanding is experienced like a reflection of light that comes from the Lord and is seen through the events of history which, illuminated by faith, become clearer and can be understood differently.

The difference between a Christian who sees the events of history in the light of faith and a non-believer is comparable to someone who can read and another who cannot. A person who cannot read can hold a book upside down without this making any difference because the signs on the pages make no sense to him. But a person with a minimal reading capacity can interpret these signs and find their meaning. In the same manner, a reading of concrete historic events illuminated by faith reveals the divine plan. With the discovery of the plan of God in history, one's own concrete responsibility

25

becomes clear. We can compare this to the strong light that we see in front of us at this moment. It is too strong to be looked at directly; we cannot perceive its meaning and we need a divine reflection to understand it. There are also moments when we do not understand the meaning of this light, not because it does not have any, but because of the limitations of our capacity of perception.

As our diocese began to move after the Council in a determined direction toward making an option for the poor--which for us was a practical obligation much more than a theoretical option because the population of our diocese is 75-78% Indigenous, poor among the poor--things began to happen. There was some criticism and worries about the new direction, and on many occasions I thought of myself as a blind man leading the blind. But when we realized that the light of faith that led us through the Council to take certain concrete steps in response to our circumstances is the same light that is leading us now, and as we saw that other processes in different contexts are also advancing, even getting ahead of us along the same path, and being led by the same light, we then said: the Spirit is blowing and we are part of this broader movement. We felt that we were in this movement in communion with other diocesan churches and this gave us a feeling of strength, peace and hope.

Faith is like a guiding light. Sometimes it is too strong for our human eyes, and we are thus incapable of perceiving its meaning. But if we continue to follow it, eventually we understand better. Without this light, the Christian could be lost. I believe that even though people of faith--as long as they let themselves be guided by the light of faith and are prepared to continue the journey--might not see their road clearly, but as long as they are going in the direction of the guiding light, they will eventually see the full vista. Faith provides peace of mind and assures hope for the future.

J. S. S.: And what would be some of your new learnings on this path of faith?

Don Samuel: There was a historic moment in the Church of my generation, which you might have known briefly, when life in society was tranquil. There were no big transformations; life was the same every day, and all the days of the week also were the same because not much happened. Life was still. Any small and insignificant event made news because nothing was happening. At that moment, faith was like a series of formulas that we applied to reality. Vatican II transformed this situation and put the emphasis back on a vision of faith which is lived in history: God speaks to us through the events of history, as the document *Dei Verbum* noted. We began to realize that God speaks to us through words and events, and that reading both is necessary to understand God's work in our history.

That is when we first began to interpret the events of history in the light of our faith. Guided later by the way the campesino and the Indigenous live their faith in concrete situations, we got to a point where, instead of applying our formulas of faith to their reality, we began to rethink our theological categories and practice in light of their reality. I believe this was a great transformation for us. In a way, it was not new; it was a return to the past, to the life of the people of God and how they were led and discovered God's presence in history. We could say that faith for us became linked to the reading of the signs of the times; that is, reading what God is saying to us through the events of our history so that we know how to move forward. I believe this is a fundamental point.

Another point, which is also not new but which we understand now with more clarity, is that the word of God has structural implications. The option for the poor, for example, is not understood to be merely an option for the poor person as an individual, rather, it is an option to change the structures that generate poverty. Pope John XXIII made this very clear in the days before the opening of the Council, when he said that the Church has to reflect on its position in relation to the world of poverty and the developing world. This implied that the Church did not have the right approach then. It is the situation of poverty in the world which led the Church to reflect on its reality and vocation. If the Church does not assume the right position in relation to the world of poverty, then it is not doing what it is supposed to do. Being in the right position leads the Church in its totality to reflect on the position it should take towards the world of poverty and the developing peoples, not only towards poor Christians. The discovery that poverty is systemic and not only a matter of poor individuals whom we need to help with fasting, alms giving, and keeping them company, made us begin to realize that we need to work to uproot the poverty caused by a social structure which is a human creation. I believe this was another discovery: structural poverty is a pointer and a necessary parameter for the Church to consider in order to determine which path to take in history.

J. S. S.: Can you to talk a little bit about your experience of dialogue with non-believers who do not necessarily have a faith position, but who do have a concern for social justice and peacemaking? How do you understand the experience of these people, their participation and contribution?

Don Samuel: I have a story to tell you about a personal experience which explains this point. At the end of my period of study in Rome, I went on a trip by boat from Italy to Egypt and from there to the Holy Land. On the boat, I met a Brazilian with whom I began to have a conversation as soon as our ship left the harbor. On the boat, you first get the sensation of being taken away from a situation where you were connected and then you find yourself as if in a nutshell in the midst of the infinite horizon, in a sea of water without limits. This nutshell keeps moving away from the land and eventually you find yourself alone and begin to chat with those who are near you. Conversations begin in a spontaneous way with the people around you, no matter who they are or where they come from and whether you know them or not. We began chatting and became acquainted a little bit. I saw my Brazilian friend again on the following day reading a covered book. I came closer to him and asked about what he was reading. "It is a book of poems by Pablo Neruda," he answered. "What do you think of this," he added. I said, "Oh, this is tragic poetry. I do not understand how someone can live with such thoughts." This was the beginning of a profound, never-ending discussion.

I had just finished my studies in Rome in theology and biblical studies and was theologically well-equipped. However, I could not in several hours of discussion with this man, and with two of his friends who joined us later, come to an agreement on anything--not even on the terms we were using. My vocabulary was incomprehensible to them. They were living in a post-war existentialism and a fatalist philosophy, believing that God did not ask for their permission to create them, and therefore they were subjected to a fatality of existence. I did not understand how people like them could go on with their lives carrying such a burden. But they were living and did not decide to end their lives. I did not understand what kept them going. We talked from five in the afternoon until three in the morning and I still did not understand why each word I said had a different meaning for them. This incident worried me a lot and made me ask questions about the possibilities of dialogue with the world if we do not even have a common language to understand each other; not even when we try to explain ourselves are we able to find common names for the issues we are discussing and agree on the meaning of the words we use.

Time passed by quickly and a few years later I found myself in this diocese. There was already a line of thinking in Mexico represented by people such as Don Sergio Méndez Arceo, Bishop of Cuernavaca, among other bishops, who were very committed to dialogue with so-called non-believers or atheists. Through their word and testimony, they had generated a movement of rapprochement with many people of that kind across the continent. Later we witnessed a similar phenomenon which emerged here in our diocese as well. The testimony of a church that tries to live charity translated into concrete actions makes a strong impact on all people. A few days ago we had visitors from Canada who were here in the northern zone of Chiapas.

They saw the difficult situation of the region and also witnessed the persecution of our diocesan church. They were moved by what they saw, and told us later during a moment of sharing, that they could easily become Catholics here. That does not mean that we are exceptional people, but when the communities here live their faith, others feel it because it is not only a conviction that stays in their heads, but it also moves down to their hearts and translates into commitment to their neighbour. This has always been our experience. Many people who visited here have told us that they were atheist, but they only got their name from atheism because when we begin to talk we agree on the substance of our commitment.

What the Council [Vatican II] stated in this regard, which only became clear to us in light of our later experience, is that there are different degrees of belonging to the Church and that non-believers also have the grace of God and can live a life of charity. It is precisely this living in charity that connects us to the spirit of the Church and is the sign of the way of salvation. I received letters from people who indicated that they did not believe but were happy to be here and would like to help with this work. These are powerful experiences for us and I do not believe that this is a unique situation. Wherever such signs exist, there the hand of the Lord is present in the work that is being done and knowing this gives us strength in our work.

The testimony of the people of faith is a witness that makes others say: "Here is a church that we want to be part of." They say this because they experience faith and a spirit of justice. They realize that there is a space here where they can revive, practice and strengthen their faith. The reaction of the people in the case of the imprisonment and liberation of Father Joel is a good example.[1] Plans were made to see how we could create more pressure to free this Church from the oppression it was undergoing. We can never say that our efforts alone

---

[1] Father Joel Padrón, parish priest of Simojovel, was detained by Mexican authorities on September 18, 1991, and released on November 6, 1991, because of a wide mobilization of the communities and organizations of the diocese.

produced the pressure we witnessed; it was much more than what our plans and efforts could generate. There is always the extra help that comes from the presence of God. The Pueblo Creyente (The People of Faith movement) emerged at a moment when we were very timid in our plans and were not able even to create a minimal structure to support and accompany the people of God in finding ways to reflect on and strengthen their faith in their various options of commitment in the popular movements and political parties. We did not have enough imagination for this. We thought that maybe we could start with groups in the parishes, and then this would develop into something bigger. But the ongoing aggression against the diocese brought people together and gave them courage to reflect and react in a quick and mature manner. It was the people themselves who created the process that in the final analysis was the decisive factor in liberating Father Joel. And the Pueblo Creyente emerged as a movement among the people of God whom we now accompany, sometimes with difficulty because they are often ahead of us. When we talk to them we feel a bit timid because they have more maturity than we do. I believe this process emerged as a result of the difficult historic moments in which we are living at the moment.

J. S. S.: What does it mean to be a prophet?

Don Samuel: Well, you are provoking me here to tackle a theoretico-practical question. Etymologically, the word prophet comes from "*pro femi*," to speak in place of someone else. It simply means someone who is the voice of, or who speaks for another person. When Moses asked God how he could speak for God when he had a stutter, God's answer to him was: "Do not be afraid, Aaron your brother will be your prophet and he will speak for you." But it is clear that this word evolved and acquired a new meaning. The word "prophet" is commonly understood to signify the person who speaks in God's name, the one whom God chooses for this task, and this choice is made in various ways. Historically, some persons were called in a very clear manner. One prophet said that he was called while he was still in his mother's womb. Others felt called for a specific task and had to leave aside all that they were doing, such as Isaiah for example. So these prophets were called by God in different ways. At one point in history, there were schools where prophets were trained. But the meaning of the word evolved with time. In the gospel, the great prophet, the highest prophet, is Christ. He did not only speak the word of God, he was the Word of God.

All Christians receive through baptism the calling to speak the word of God. We are called to witness to God primarily through our way of life, and therefore, in a certain sense, we are all prophets. Some are called to free themselves and become totally dedicated to speak the Word of God and to give witness to the community. This is a service to the community which is recognized and agreed upon within the Christian community. God speaks to us in different ways, but through Christ, God spoke to us a definitive word which we are called to communicate, that is to announce the Reign of God. As we do this, we are in this sense speaking the word of God and therefore we are prophets: we speak in God's name. All the baptized are given this mission and calling. Sometimes it happens that one person in the community emerges in a special way as someone whose word is listened to and contemplated as a word that comes from God to the community. This kind of prophecy has been historically exercised and recognized by the Church. In time, the usage of the word evolved and the name prophet was given not only to those who speak the word of God, but also to those who tell the future: things such as announcing an eventual liberation of a people, or the foretelling of an imminent catastrophe so that people can reflect and change their ways. With this perception, the word acquired a new meaning, which is that of announcing the future.

Saint Paul counts prophecy among the gifts of the Spirit to the Church and to the individual Christian, and according to him, it is not totally separated from the task of announcing the future. Prophecy is not usually an extraordinary illumination: it is the observation of events of history in concrete situations, using our human faculties and a faith perspective so that we can read in these events the plan of God and announce it; it is the announcement of the Reign of God in these situations. This is what it means to speak in God's name and this is, I believe, what it means to be a prophet today. Prophecy acquires a special importance when someone is speaking for a group of people who do not have a voice. In this case, speaking for the poor, for example, whose word represents the word of Christ, is also an act of prophecy.

J. S. S.: Why did you choose "So that you build and plant" from the prophet Jeremiah as a motto for your Episcopal ordination?

Don Samuel: Sometimes certain things can get mystified and become a motive for a long exegesis, but the reason behind this choice was very simple. We had to choose a motto in a short time before the celebration of my Episcopal ordination, and two Monsignors who were involved in the preparation of the ceremony with the sisters suggested this passage from Jeremiah. It sounded good to me and it felt right for the historic moment then. We were just coming out of a period of religious persecution in the aftermath of the Mexican Revolution, which was seen as a time of destruction. This is expressed in the first part of this verse from Jeremiah "I send you to uproot and destroy." After destruction comes the time for restoration, which is expressed in the second half of the same passage, "to build and plant." They thought of this and proposed it to me with a brief exegesis saying that the time of destruction has passed and it was now time to plant and build. But I also believe that this passage carried a vision which transcended that moment. We had then just begun the preparations for Vatican II, which had not yet been announced, whose spirit was also to build and edify. The Council had to face the dawn of a new world, decide how the Church can play a role in it and, and open the doors for the Church to be present in history--to be inside the events of history, not to just preach from the outside hoping this would influence the world. That is, the Church had to recognize the presence of God in history and to go on announcing and advancing the Reign of God in it.

Time passed. In a providential manner, and as a result of the Council, and in the same spirit, we became involved here in the planting and edifying of the autochthonous churches among the Indigenous communities, who form the majority in our diocese. We became aware of this reality as we began to reflect on the incarnated evangelization after the Council. One of the main contributions of the Council was that it prepared the way for the subsequent concrete reflections on the Latin American Church that took place in Medellín. It was there that we talked about the option for the poor, and for the poorest among the poor.

J. S. S.: I was imagining myself as a disciple coming before his master and asking him: How can I become a prophet? What do I need to do?

Don Samuel: Unlike biblical times, we do not nowadays have schools for prophets; otherwise I would have told you to go and register in such or such a school and they would teach you. I believe the Apostle Peter provides us with a key for answering this question. He told us to let ourselves be guided by the word the Lord inspires in our heart (*tocibiles dei*). We need to let ourselves be guided and taught by events and concrete historical situations, asking at each moment what it is that God wants from us now. And, we must understand that faith is lived in relation with the other, because we cannot love God separately from our neighbour. Saint John understood this as complete charity. Those who say that they love God and do not love their brother or sister, he said, are lying and living in illusion. We cannot make a profession of love to God, without including our neighbour. Jesus Christ, the incarnated Son of God, changed the relationship between God and humanity. After Jesus, we cannot love God directly leaving aside the love of our neighbour. The Ten Commandments taught that the love of God and of our neighbour, although related, were still two things. But Jesus responded to a question put to him by a master of the law by saying that there are two fundamental commandments of equal value: love of God, and love of our neighbour. By saying this, Jesus joined together the two previous commandments; love of God and of our neighbour become united and it is through loving our neighbour that we love God. Our profession of faith is intimately united to love of our neighbour and we cannot love God directly. Love of our neighbour is what makes the love of God grow within us. It is by nurturing this love that we begin to discover the plan God has for us and how we can know what God is asking of us at a certain moment.

Being a prophet is nothing more than making our life a witness to what we believe in. This is what it means to proclaim the Reign of God. In certain specific circumstances, we might be asked to dedicate ourselves and take more responsibility for important things in the process of change. This requires giving testimony, and with this might even come persecution for the Lord's name. This additional cost of suffering is a necessary mark of following the Lord. A prophet and follower of Christ who has not suffered as a result of this would have no guarantee that the message he is proclaiming is authentic. The test of the prophetic message is the suffering for the Lord which comes with it. This is a clear indication that we are following God and proclaiming God's word. I believe that being prophets calls us to be consistent in what we believe and how we live this out. That is the most effective proclamation of the Reign of God.

J. S. S.: What is the place of mysticism in the political commitment of Christians?

Don Samuel: The bishops of the southern pacific region [of Mexico] wrote a pastoral letter a few years ago in which there is a section that touches on your question.[2] I believe what we said in that letter is still valid today. People who do politics as an option of their faith, who make an impact on concrete historical situations as they search for change, and who proclaim and build the Reign of God in truth and justice, come to the realization that this work cannot be done without a payment of suffering. This is the cost of following Jesus who said: "If you want to come after me, take up your cross and follow me."

When we follow Jesus in our efforts to realize political change in its various manifestations, whether in organizing political actions which involve the community, or in actions with a political party in the city (in a selective way), etc., if these actions are done in a Christian spirit, they will lead to misunderstanding, persecution and suffering which is characteristic of following Jesus. In following this path, one will experience the isolation and misunderstanding that Jesus suffered at certain significant moments in his life which hold a great mystery: "My Father, why have you forsaken me!" Feeling misunderstood by everyone and feeling deep loneliness, is a profound mystical moment. It is mystical and also has a sense of mystery; it feels as if one is journeying in darkness, without clarity. In addition to that comes the suffering of persecution, defamation, and a psychological assassination of the person; that is when, as a result of defamation and slander, one is cut off from the possibility of social relations. This isolation and suffering, added to a journey through danger, facing persecution and unjust imprisonment as a part of the solidarity with and the accompaniment of the other--that is, a punishment inflicted on someone not because of an individual misdeed, but rather as revenge against a new political awareness and concientization that is emerging in society; all this becomes a profound mystical experience.

---

[2]Obispos de la Región Pacifico Sur, *Vivir Cristianamente el Compromiso Politico* (Bishops of the South-Pacific Region, Living our Political Commitment as Christians), Diocese of San Cristóbal de Las Casas, 1982.

J. S. S.: Remembering your fast in December of 1994 as a response to the interruption of the dialogue [between the Mexican government and the EZLN] and to the increasing probability of a renewed armed conflict, I would like to ask you in this context if you could share with us some of your reflections on prayer, fasting and alms giving, all being important practices which have always been part of the life of the Church?

Don Samuel: I believe the meanings of these religious expressions have had different emphases at various moments in history--not contradictory meanings, but different interpretations and ways for living them out. For the Christian, these practices were never meant to be for exclusive personal purposes. Fasting, for example, was never meant to be a form of self-punishment, or penance for individual sins or for personal purification for following the Lord. This is a misunderstanding of fasting. Since biblical times, fasting was seen in relation to one's neighbour, not centered on the self and personal purification, which are not excluded but were never the focus of fasting. In the Middle Ages, it is said that fasting went through an interesting development. During Lent, it was customary to invite any poor person who knocked at one's door into the dining room and seat him at the head of the table. Many people believed that the Lord was present in the poor person knocking at the door and that this person should be invited to eat with the family and be given a place of honour. Fasting, therefore, was linked to this practice. Today, we see a structural interpretation of the meaning of fasting. Lent has become a time for collecting donations to help the Third World and support projects which are a sign and expression of the restoration of justice.

In my situation, I was thinking together with other people and asking for advice--although the final decision was personal--about what could be done to open new ways for dialogue in the impasse we were experiencing. The idea of fasting arose. It was also a sign of confidence in a spiritual practice whose efficacy is not known to many people today. The solidarity we experienced during this fast, not only from this continent but also from overseas, was very impressive. We felt the spiritual power of this expression of repentance like a powerful invasion which deterred the imminent confrontation between two armies [the Mexican Army and the Zapatistas], a confrontation which would have changed the face of our country. I believe it was a moment of faith and hope which became an opportunity for an outpouring of solidarity from the Lord, and which helped us to advance in our search for a new path for peace.

Alms-giving is not about boasting in public about helping a neighbour in need. It is instead a sign of the efforts being done to change the situation that generates poverty. Today we are clear about the fact that the world of the poor and the world of the rich do not exist independently of each other. Instead, they are rather interdependent: there is wealth in some parts because there is poverty in other parts. There is a relationship in the prevailing system between depredation and devastation. Therefore, we must act in such a way as to not let the necessary help we give to our neighbour in a particular situation of need make us forget that we have also to help him to eliminate the causes that brought about this situation of poverty, and to find alternatives. We know that as we are trying to make great efforts to help one person recover from poverty, at the same time thousands of others are being drawn by the system into poverty. Therefore, the sign and witness of giving should be a motivation for us to search with more determination for solidarity.

Some religious congregations are re-thinking their vows in light of this new meaning. The vow of poverty is a protest in face of this unjust world order which creates poverty. Making a vow for poverty is assuming the cause of the poor and making an option for the poor within the Church so that the Church does not only favour the cause of the poor, and does not only act in solidarity with them, but also becomes poor with the poor. In this sense, the Church will help in the construction of a social structure that is based on sharing instead of accumulation, and by doing this, it will contribute to make austerity part of the structure of the new world which the Church is promoting, a world where authentic sharing and equality become a real possibility.

J. S. S.: I see the conclusion of this section as an invitation to prayer so that we can be profoundly united in our commitment to a Christian witness of hope at this historic moment.

Don Samuel: Indeed. What you just called prayer and witness are two things which cannot be taken separately. Jesus said: "Not every one who says to me 'Lord, Lord,' shall enter the kingdom of heaven, only those who do the will of my Father." Prayer, therefore, sustains, helps, and strengthens our commitment; prayer and commitment are intimately connected. If we bring our offering to the altar, says the Lord, and it is not accompanied by a commitment to the service of our neighbour--especially the poor, our offering is not acceptable. This is a fundamental precondition.

III - FAITH AND POLITICS

J. S. S.: Is there a conflict between faith and politics?

Don Samuel: The question needs clarification because people have different assumptions about the meaning of politics. [...] We have to first define what is understood by politics, and then see whether doing this kind of politics is in conflict with Christian faith.

In principle, we can say that a citizen who is a Christian would have no conflict between his or her faith and political action. Vatican II affirmed that it is lay people who have the task of making the Reign of God more concrete in history, and by doing this the Council opened the door for Christians to become involved in politics. So, there is clearly openness to political action. This could take the form of participation in direct actions, which are intended to transform society, or by joining movements which aim to improve specific aspects of the political structure or even to change the political structure. Or, this also could be done through active participation in larger political movements such as political parties. This becomes politics in the broad sense--general politics--and in this case, we have to make sure that the actions of the individuals concerned have an impact on the *polis*, on the city and society as a whole, and that they are not done for the party's or the individual's own sake.

Every action can be a political action: thinking, writing a poem, or going for a walk. ... When I preach--no matter what the topic may be, even if it is about mysticism-- and it touches the people and helps them to become actors in society, then this is a political act. Every act that motivates people and calls on the individual to participate in the process of social transformation to make society a better place, is a political act. There can also be a political reading of any social group in society. In our diocese, for example, we have about 8,000 catechists in the communities and their presence has an impact on transforming society. In this sense, this could be characterized as a political group. If the notion of politics is reduced to only party politics in the strict sense, then in this case we see potential conflicts if members of the church hierarchy are involved in politics. Even without an official position which prohibits them from becoming involved in party politics, priests and religious, by the nature of their function as part of the hierarchical structure of the Church in one way or another, place a restriction upon themselves as regards involvement in party politics.

What is at stake here is the unity of the church and the community. The primary task of the bishop, the priest, and those who represent the church at a certain moment in their community, is to work for the unity of their community. This is a universal call and it cannot be done through a partisan political movement because these groups, by their nature, separate people. No one party can bring all people together, not even those who vote for the same party. Members of a specific political party, by the act of belonging to that party, separate themselves from others who have chosen another way of thinking and participation in society.

The Reign of God is universal. It is for all. People are illuminated by their faith to act within society and make their own decisions. The political choice of an individual Christian, or a group of Christians, which is illuminated by their faith, has to be consistent with their faith. They should also try to make the objectives and actions of their party adequately congruous with their Christian faith. Otherwise they are living in falsehood and hypocrisy.

If, in the process of building the Reign of God, we take action which has a political dimension, we must never lose sight of the task of maintaining the unity of the community--a primary function of the Church hierarchy. This work for unity should be kept in mind before, during, and after making political choices so as not to generate divisions and animosities instead of searching for the unity and common good of the community. We see conflicts and divisions arising around those who want to take a position of leadership and responsibility for the unity of the community while at the same time continuing to be militant partisan activists. Joining a political party as such is not a bad thing, but then one cannot at the same time fulfill a specific function in the community which has as its primary responsibility building and maintaining the unity of that community.

J. S. S.: Faith, then, puts certain demands on us in terms of our commitment to the human person, to society, and to ourselves, of which political commitment is only one expression. Sometimes there is a conflict between political commitment, the exercise of power that comes with it and service to the community. What is your opinion on the matter?

Don Samuel: I can only respond to this question from my own experience. The way Jesus understood society and founded his Church calls into question the exercise of power as a form of domination. We learn from Jesus that in the society of his time, some people were using the power entrusted to them to dominate other people rather than to serve them. Jesus criticized their practice, and the way he contemplated and exercised power was different. "I was given all power in heaven and on earth," he said to his disciples, and he used this power in the service of the Reign of God and the gospel--that is for service and not for domination. This is precisely where the potential conflict lies and our human nature is susceptible to this temptation.

The Apostle Paul, following the word of Jesus, gives a clear example on the exercise of power. He makes an analogy between the practice of power in the community and the members of the human body. Each member performs a proper function in the service of the whole body: the eyes have the power of sight but they do not keep this for themselves; the eyes see so that the feet, the lowest part of the body, can walk. The feet cannot walk if the eyes do not see, and sight is useless if it is not put at the service of the whole body. In a similar manner, power in the community should be exercised as a service to the whole community, not for the benefit of a few.

It is clear that society, including the Church at times, is structured in such a way as to exercise domination. The documents of Vatican II draw our attention to this structure and call for a return to a practice of power as service. It suggests that the use of symbols and signs inside the Church structure, such as dress and the way of relating to people, should reflect an attitude of fraternity and service. Inside the Christian community, power has no reason to exist if it is not for service. Vatican II also indicated that Church authorities should exercise their power as service. The idea of forming pastoral councils to assist in the leadership of the community was suggested so that just one person does not impose his will over others, and to guarantee that authority is exercised as service. The documents of Puebla, the meeting of the Latin American bishops after Vatican II and Medellín, indicated that a Church which make an option for the poor, and which by the same act tries to get rid of its power of domination and instead exercise power as service, should modify its structure in such a way as to allow the poor the possibility of taking positions of leadership inside its structure; that is, making it possible for humble and simple people to speak their word and participate in the decision making process. The optimal situation would be to have shared leadership to ensure that power is exercised in the service of the progress of the community.

J. S. S.: In the context of your ministry of mediation with the CONAI at the present moment, do you experience any difficulties in the exercise of power as service and power as direction and authority?[1]

---

[1]CONAI is the National Mediation Commission which had the role of a mediator in the dialogue for peace between the Zapatista National Liberation Army (EZLN) and the Mexican government from 1994-1998. Bishop Ruiz was the president of CONAI during all this period.

Don Samuel: No, there is no conflict between my ministry and the service of mediation I am performing. On the contrary, my ministry has helped the service of mediation--not only in a symbolic way--and had a real impact on national society. We already know that even though the conflict began here in Chiapas, it has a national dimension, whether this is admitted or not. The attention that has been given to the so-called Chiapas phenomenon, in Mexico and abroad, is an obvious indication. Therefore, this opportunity to provide a broad platform in the service of mediation was never in conflict with our pastoral mission and ministry. We always understood that our pastoral work is not only directed to Christians, it is addressed to the whole of society, including of course the Christian community. All that we do is for the benefit of the mystical body of Christ. In this sense, there was never a conflict between the work of mediation we are doing and our conscience. We already knew as a diocese many years ago--long before the conflict [with the Zapatistas]--that our work is not limited by the boundaries of the Catholic Church, despite its universality. Our pastoral work has reached beyond the Church, and our ministry to the Indigenous communities, the poorest of our people, has transcended the ecclesial boundaries of our diocese and has had repercussions abroad.

Bearing all this in mind, it was no surprise to us to see that the ministry of mediation we were asked to do has had a much broader dimension than our diocese. We are aware at the moment of the fact that, as a diocese, we are promoting a ministry of reconciliation in Chiapas and beyond. In this too, we do not experience any conflict with our conscience. We do experience conflict with those in power who do not always perceive their exercise of power as service and who want to manipulate the process of mediation. According to them, our mediation is not neutral because we speak the truth. In their opinion, a neutral mediation should be blind and mute; that is we should not see the truth, and if we see injustice we should not talk about it, otherwise, we are not neutral. This kind of neutrality, we believe, is not evangelical. Neutrality according to the gospel is to be

44

on the side of justice and truth, and not to be partial in their interpretation.

J. S. S.: As a Christian, where does your sense of freedom come from? How do you bring together your search for freedom and being a Christian?

Don Samuel: I was asked the same question not long ago and at first it surprised me. I was at a meeting of the Latin American Dominicans where I was asked to talk a little bit about the work of the Dominicans of our diocese in Ocosingo.[2] I spoke about how the proclamation of the gospel in our diocese took on a more concrete historical dimension after Vatican II, and how this Council returned to the gospel its primitive original splendor. After this short presentation, which touched on a whole range of things, three persons approached me and asked questions similar to what you are asking me now: "How is it that you are capable of saying what you think? From where do you get the strength to freely tell things as they are, and to do that without fear?" Another added to it by asking me whether it is possible to do what we say! I think he meant to ask whether there is consistency between what we say and what we do.

I believe there is no other source for this freedom than the gospel which has clearly indicated that "The truth shall make you free." If our search for the truth is sincere--knowing well that we never possess the full truth--and if we place ourselves in a position which allows us to continue to be open to dialogue with others, we experience a sense of freedom that comes with this. There is certainly a price to pay for speaking the truth. When we speak the truth, by the same act we become committed to it. Speaking the truth has some concrete implications on our lives. We cannot be living in a situation contradictory to what we have said; we cannot live in the truth by simply saying it and expecting others to live it out. Our deeds have to

---

[2]Ocosingo is a region of the diocese of San Cristóbal where the Dominicans have had a missionary presence since the early 1960s.

45

be consistent with what we say. What also becomes a source of great freedom is the fact that we are not working for and expecting a reward from the people around us. The main concern is the answer that one has to give before the Lord of history; it is about the final and definitive true response we give to the God of history and which begins with the positions we take here and now. I believe this is what gives us the freedom of the spirit: knowing that our response and responsibility are not just to situations and history, but that the judge to whom we are accountable knows our heart, and is also accompanying us on our journey in history.

J. S. S.: This sense of freedom is also felt among many pastoral workers. What permitted this exercise of freedom in the diocese?

Don Samuel: I believe that one does not need to ask for permission to be free. This is a human right, isn't it? In a way, we, the older generation in the diocese, have been through a process together. Freedom was not something that was granted to us; we built it as we lived and we worked together to achieve it. It was the fruit of a communal effort and it is a common acquisition. We are free because we speak the truth. We earned this freedom, it was not given to us.

We are also free because we maintained our independence from the civil authorities, even though they tried hard on several occasions to buy us. We never accepted presents, such as a car, or the painting of our public facilities, or any personal gifts or favours that came with conditions attached. This is what helped us to keep our freedom. This freedom of the spirit allowed us to be critical of others and of ourselves: if we have the freedom to see, act and say things from the point of view of the gospel, by the same act, this process makes us realize our own failures and critique our own actions.

J. S. S.: Do you feel isolated?

Don Samuel: I believe that the complexity of our unique social situations in the diocese made us realize from the outset that we can never have an appropriate pastoral plan without the participation of those concerned. It was up to them to make their own analysis and decide on how they want to respond. After the Indigenous Congress [1974] we began to move forward in our pastoral response to the concrete needs of the communities because the Congress provided a framework for our pastoral action, the proclamation of the gospel, and the building of the Reign of God. In all this, we were naturally sharing the responsibility with many people from the Indigenous communities who themselves became aware of the needs of their communities and the necessity of a response; we were collaborating with them and not working on our own. When we are all implicated in the work together, we do not feel isolated; there is a real sense of journeying together. That is the reality of our situation. If all the responsibility of the diocesan pastoral work were on my shoulders and I had to make all the decisions and say the last word on everything, then I would not only feel isolated, but overwhelmed. The situation is very complex and there are serious difficulties. The responsibility is not shared just for the sake of sharing, but because there is a need for sharing and for more wisdom. I believe this was the way to go for us so that we can have freedom and peace of spirit and not feel isolated. In addition, when we see that other dioceses, who might have been living in different historical contexts, have also taken positions similar to ours, and sometimes have even surpassed us, we rejoice and feel that we all are guided by the light of the same Spirit on our journey as we try to give a relevant answer to history. This makes us feel not only not isolated, but we also feel the joy of solidarity and the catholicity of the Church.

J. S. S.: One last question: what would be some of the aspects of the spiritual testimony and legacy that we are leaving to history and to those who come after us, who share the same commitment

and search for peacemaking and the construction of a new society?

Don Samuel: There are many aspects to this question which opens a variety of horizons. I believe the experience of our diocese has been tested. The other day at a meeting of the pastoral workers, we clearly witnessed an expression of a generalized gratitude because our service to the poor gives us a great freedom of the spirit, fills us with joy and nurtures our faith. We discovered the mystery of the Lord revealed to the poor. This was the surprise the Lord had for us and which many of us have witnessed. "I give you thanks, O Father, for you have revealed these things to the humble and the poor of heart." Also, the way the word of God is being lived in the Indigenous and campesino communities has had a profound impact on us. We announced this word to them, but the way they lived it out made it rebound and transform us. I will give you a recent example.

In the northern zone we have serious problems at the moment which are interpreted by some authorities in such a way as to make it sound as if we are the ones who are causing the violence. This situation forced many people to leave their communities. Some of them had family members who became victims, and in addition to that, they are now suffering the consequences of repression. They were forced to leave their communities with their chapel burned, its images profaned, and the consecrated host thrown on the floor; they were taken away from their homes and reality, warned not to come back to harvest their crops, and they have no place to go where they can meet and celebrate as a community. They sent us a letter saying that they were not allowed to come and be with us at this time. They mentioned in their letter how they were all encouraged when they shared the word of God. They were motivated by their living faith in these moments of suffering to not give up and to continue to move ahead with the same enthusiasm as before.

Well, when a suffering person or community, which has been displaced for more than a month and cannot return, which is enduring serious sicknesses caused by hunger, lack of basic food and medication, and which is not allowed to move freely in any direction, is yet able to say, in the midst of all these sufferings, that their faith and their courage did not faint, this clearly indicates the depth of their faith. The true and authentic inner consolation they feel, and the joy of continuing on the path of faith despite the suffering, are incomprehensible to us. But this is something that we are all witnessing. We have the great treasure of the poor among us; we accompany them believing that to them belongs the Reign of Heaven. Their common action was born with the hope of advancement, leaving behind misery and deprivation to build a new life, not only for themselves, but for all of us; a new society of sharing of all goods and of living in true fraternity. This is the message that we received from them. We have realized, in truth, that rather than us evangelizing the poor, it is the poor who, receiving the word of the Lord, are evangelizing us.

Another aspect of our pastoral experience is community life and action which is a way of life that gives security and strength. Acting together does not simply mean the total sum of individual efforts in an arbitrary way, but it is bringing together the insights which help us determine which path we should follow. This is a source of great richness which gives freedom of the spirit, because we know that it is not only our personal thoughts and feelings that we are following, it is what became clear to us as a community that led us to take action together. This community action and journeying together in light of the word of the Lord is truly a source of great joy. We have been walking together in this manner, and without realizing it, our action has had an impact beyond our diocese. People from our diocese are generally welcome in many places--sometimes rejected in some-- and our work is perceived as a positive historic sign of hope. This reception, and this feeling of living in a much larger community than our diocese gives us the assurance that we are following the Lord. We realize that we are enduring a lot of suffering at the present moment-- which could have also been brought upon us as a result of our mistakes--but when our intention is to follow Jesus, this suffering unites us with many others and fills us with joy. We now understand what it means when the Lord says: "My burden is light and my yoke is easy."

J. S. S.: Thank you very much Don Samuel. It has been a great experience for me to be able to share these reflections with you.

Don Samuel: This conversation makes me want to interview you too and listen to your reading of this history and experience in which you also took part. I believe that the questions you asked were coming from your personal experience of this process. Your experience in prison, for example, living in darkness for several days without really knowing what you were charged with, this condemnation of innocence and life alongside other people who might be in similar or different circumstances but who were all deprived of external freedom, I believe this is a unique experience that must have marked your Christian faith and life.

J. S. S.: Yes, it was a very significant experience for me.

Don Samuel: I said to Father Joel when I first saw him in prison: "Your word now will have much more power because this experience will make you more credible." He said: "No, now I have become a word, and an event. Whether I talk or not, what happened is already a testimony." Later in our conversation he explained this further to me saying that he had an extraordinary feeling in prison: being behind bars was supposed to take away his freedom and isolate him from the outside world, but during his time in prison, he said, he felt less isolated than at any time in his life. These were powerful words which cannot be contained by prison bars.

APPENDIX I

PEACE, MEDIATION AND THE ROLE OF THE CHURCHES

*Excerpts from an interview with Bishop Samuel Ruiz
conducted by Jorge Santiago and Michel Andraos
San Cristóbal de Las Casas, July 1997*

Q: Can we talk about an emerging theology of peace as a result of your pastoral work of mediation?

Don Samuel: Contrary to how people in the North think or expect, we do not have an elaborated thinking on the theology of peace. There is no theology of peace as such; there are reflections on our pastoral practice. Our work for peace is not the result of an elaborated theology that we try to apply. We are responding to a concrete situation of conflict and we reflect as we respond, but not according to an abstract, already elaborated theory. The difficulty in responding to a question like this is that you might expect an elaborated theoretical answer. Here things do not function that way; we reflect on our work of mediation as we do it and that is our theology of peace. I wanted to clarify this before answering your question. In this framework then, yes there is a work of mediation that we are doing and we reflect on it as we do it.

One of the difficulties that the work of mediation faces, here and in other conflicts, is how to make constant efforts to distance oneself from the parties in conflict which are involved in the negotiation. In our situation, we do not represent the EZLN when we talk to the government nor do we represent the government when we talk to the EZLN. We are interested in what both are thinking and we try to find a way to translate what they are trying to say to each other. We are not talking here only about linguistic translation, this is also a

51

cultural translation because we are dealing with different Indigenous communities who speak distinct native languages and have different cultures. So, first of all, there is here a problem of linguistic and cultural communication. This work of cultural interpretation is part of our work of mediation.

The risk here is that some people want to relate to us as if we were a party in the conflict--which we are not. We are not Zapatistas, we are Christians doing a collective work of mediation through the CONAI, over which I preside. I am not the mediator, I am only the coordinator of this work of mediation. The dialogue is between the EZLN and the government. We do not participate in the dialogue, we are merely linguistic and cultural interpreters and communicators in a dialogue which is part of a peace process that emerged as a result of the active participation of Mexican civil society. In El Salvador, for example, there was no active participation of civil society. There was a hope that this would happen, but it did not.

In Mexico today, there is an active presence of civil society whose representatives participate in the dialogue in various capacities, at times as advisors and also through the national forums which have taken place. In this context, our mediation has a fundamental function in the dialogue and in the relationship with civil society. This is part of the role the CONAI is trying to develop which is consistent with the initial demands of the Zapatistas, who from the very beginning of the conflict did not ask civil society to join their armed rebellion, rather they asked for civil and political democratic participation in the resolution of the conflict.

From the very beginning it was perceived that the achievement of peace would not be the result of a dialogue and signing of a peace accord with the government because of the good political will of the government, but rather as the result of the pressure and participation of civil society which is co-responsible for this peace process. From a Christian perspective we can affirm, not as a theoretical abstract statement, but based on our experience, that peace is achieved and built through the responsible participation of all citizens--it is the responsibility of all. This affirmation is not a principle or a theory that we want to apply, it is the result of a praxis which is illuminated by our faith and which has become a guiding principle. The difference between the way you asked your question and the answer is that, although we come to the same conclusion, the process is different.

We are living in a war situation. It is not an open war where people die every day in the fighting, it is a low intensity war. Therefore, talking about peace is something we do constantly. Building peace does not mean just an end to the actual fighting, it is the building of a society where there is justice, where justice and peace embrace. If the root causes of the conflict are not dealt with, there will be no peace. The causes of the conflict in Chiapas are not only local; if there were no economic system that is contributing to creating all these problems, there would have been no conflict, neither here nor in other parts of the world.

Q: You mentioned at one instance that the work of mediation and peacemaking is part of the pastoral task of the bishop and that it is an essential component of the mission and identity of the church. Can you explain a little bit more what do you mean by this affirmation?

Don Samuel: Our work of mediation began as a response to a concrete situation. I was invited along with two other people who could not accept this task because of their particular situation, so I stayed by myself, but from the outset the intention was to have a national committee for mediation. It was clear to me from the beginning that I would not have accepted this task if I did not see it as a service related to my pastoral work; I would not have accepted it if it were strictly a political task, even if it is not partisan. My work of mediation has a political dimension but it is not only political. I was not initially invited for political reasons; this was clear to me and to the diocese. I was invited because I have 37 years of pastoral work and presence here. It is in this capacity, and because of the assurance my presence gives to one of the parties, that I was invited to do this work of mediation; it is an extension of the pastoral work of accompaniment the diocese has already been doing.

Another point which is related to mediation and the work of the church is our understanding that the Reign of God and its justice are central to our work of evangelization. The role of the Church is to announce and work for the realization of the Reign of God--without identifying itself with this Reign. It is important that our pastoral work become concrete in this task of building the Reign of God through the restoration of justice and order. Only this way can we attain a true and authentic peace that responds to the root causes of the rebellion which is precisely the result of a situation of oppression and injustice. From this perspective, mediation is an important element on which we have reflected in light of our Christian faith and in the context of the building of the Reign of God in our specific situation. This concrete proclamation and building of the Reign of God is an essential part of the task of the bishop and the Church. We made it clear to the Mexican Conference of Catholic Bishops from the beginning that we were not going to do anything which is not within the bounds of our pastoral work. I told them that the moment my work of mediation becomes exclusively political, it will cease.

The work of mediation is the work of the whole diocese. It is also a task of reconciliation in the divided communities as a result of old tensions activated and exacerbated by new external factors which were artificially imposed on them. Working for reconciliation and the unity of the communities in this context is a pastoral task which constitutes part of our diocesan plan and action. In this sense, the work for peace in the communities is clear and concrete. It is not a vague theoretical plan for peace which is far removed from reality and which does not have concrete application. Rather, it is working in divided communities to reconcile their factions. This has been the focus of our pastoral work as a diocese at the present moment.

Q: You have said on several occasions that the present neoliberal global economic order is generating poverty, exclusion, marginalization and causing conflicts. What role do you see the churches playing in this context?

Don Samuel: We are all co-responsible to see that the present global system does not generate the injustice it is creating. There is a need for a fundamental change in the system. This is not my analysis, it is a well known fact; the Pope also said this when he was here in Yucatan in 1993. The capitalist system, which is the only system left in the world at this moment, and which has become more generalized and more efficient with globalization, is causing the gradual dispossession of many and the accumulation of economic and political power in the hands of an ever fewer number of individuals and groups. This phenomenon is happening in a more accelerated manner now in what is called the Third World which includes us here in Latin America. Here in Mexico, for example, the number of families that receive more than 70 percent of the national income has been reduced from 80 or so to maybe 14 or 15 families. Those are the only people who are competing at national and international levels. This process is rapidly affecting average people, and working in favor of the rich at the expense of the poor. Despite all this, many countries are saying that, according to their books, the economic crisis is over because they have balanced their budgets, their debt is under control and they have a surplus.

This is a question of co-responsibility between the First World and the Third World. Our economic and political problems here are not only caused by what is happening there; our local governments here play a role in the global economic game and share in the abuse of economic power. According to many analysts, one of the main reasons for the January 1, 1994 rebellion here in Chiapas was the rapid decline of the coffee price in 1993. The majority of the people in the four municipalities where the rebellion took place are small coffee producers and they have no control whatsoever over the price of their produce; the price is decided somewhere else in the international market. Of course, this was not the only cause of the rebellion, but many say it was the drop that caused the flood. The situation was already tense as a result of repression and other difficulties that the people were experiencing here in 1993. In Chiapas, we have the most delicate social strata in Mexico. The Zapatistas' rebellion was a symptom of a generalized situation which had been simmering in the whole country and it exploded here. In 1993, the Mexican political system was going through a major crisis. One could look at any newspaper on any day of that year and see the reflection of this national political crisis. It was an election year. In 17 states across the country the elected governors were rejected by their own communities because of fraud and manipulation. Many municipal buildings nationwide were occupied by the people as a sign of protest. Here in Chiapas, out of one hundred or so municipalities, seventy four were occupied by people protesting electoral fraud and imposed councils.

The system was generating all these problems. What I mean by what I referred to above as co-responsibility is that those who make the big economic decisions should share the responsibility of what is happening here in the Third World as a result of their decisions; their big decisions there have economic consequences and political repercussions here. There is a need for a fundamental revision of these decisions to correct this deteriorating situation. I have no expertise in economics, but those in this world who do, are called to make proposals and search for solutions to this situation which is causing the death of many people.

In this context we understand why the Zapatista movement attracted so much attention. It was not a movement that called people to violence and to take over the government by force. It was a shock and a protest that appealed to many people and got national, and to a certain extent international support, because it was a call for dialogue to find a solution and not a call to violence. It was a call to search in a peaceful manner for ways to change the system which is generating violence; that is the social and economic system which is causing the death of many. The question was how to find a peaceful way to change it. It is not a question of reaching a middle way solution, it is about finding new ways so that there is an equitable distribution and sharing of wealth which makes community life possible and opens a new path of life for humanity. In the new context of globalization, there is a call emerging from within the system. The way of production on which the international economic system depends is abusing natural resources and destroying the environment in a way that threatens the survival of humanity. The ecological demand, together with the demand for social justice are both urgent. What is happening in the Third World is not marginal to the rest of the world; we are all in the same boat and we need to act together to find solutions. It is in this context that we talk about international co-responsibility and the need for fundamental change in the global system.

Q: Where do you see the responsibility of the churches in this process?

Don Samuel: I prefer to speak about the responsibility of Christians rather than churches, because the term church could be ambiguous for some people who still think that the Church is the clergy and the hierarchy--even though Vatican II has clarified these issues. International co-responsibility and solidarity are tasks for all Christians. Obviously institutional support from the Church hierarchy would help, but the Pope told the Indigenous peoples who went to meet with him in Yucatan [1993] to take responsibility and initiative themselves to sólve their own problems and not to wait for others to do that for them. We are all called to do the same in our own situations without necessarily waiting for the initiative to come from the Church hierarchy.

Q: Is there international collaboration among the different Church groups involved in mediation and peacemaking to share experiences and do common theological reflections?

Don Samuel: Yes, there are some initiatives. We had a few meetings in Europe and in other places in Latin America called by the Latin American Conference of Bishops (CELAM) and the Latin American Council of Churches (CLAI), but this work is just beginning and there is a need for much more. I believe it is not only a question of making a summary of the work of mediation in various places and gathering the results together, because each place is different from the others. It is a matter of doing critical reflection on the method and process of mediation and peace building so that we can avoid the mistakes of others and learn from each other's experiences. It is not about doing theological reflections on the results, it is about reflecting critically on the process. The problem is that the people who can do this are too busy in their own situations and it is not easy for them to free themselves for this task. But this is important work that still needs to be done.

APPENDIX II

THE ATTACKS ON THE DIOCESE OF SAN CRISTOBAL, THE OPTION FOR THE POOR, THE FUTURE OF PEACE, AND INTERNATIONAL SOLIDARITY

A Conversation with Bishop Samuel Ruiz, Fray Gonzalo Ituarte and Jorge Santiago

A group of eleven members from The Canadian Catholic Organization for Development and Peace from Ontario met with Don Samuel Ruiz, bishop of the diocese of San Cristóbal de Las Casas, Fray Gonzalo Ituarte, Vicar of Justice and Peace for the diocese, and Jorge Santiago, director of DESMI, the Civil Association for Economic and Social Development of Indigenous Mexicans, in San Cristóbal de Las Casas, Chiapas, on August 18, 1998. The following is an edited translation of our conversation with them.

Can you tell us about the present attacks against the diocese of San Cristóbal?

Don Samuel: The attacks against our diocesan church are not new. They began before the conflict of 1994. In his second public statement, the governor of Chiapas, Patrocinio González Garrido [1988-1993], declared war against the Diocese, its bishop, priests, deacons, religious communities, and catechists accusing us of being enemies of the state and an obstacle to the official project of the government. In reality, we are opposed to the government's projects of destruction and injustice that are imposed on the campesino and Indigenous communities. The term of Patrocinio González Garrido ended with great oppression against the Indigenous communities. Before 1994, the opposition to the Diocese came mainly from the ranchers and the landowners. The Diocese was supporting the

Indigenous communities in denouncing human rights violations and injustices such as assassinations and other forms of violence, committed against them by some ranchers and landowners. These ranchers and landowners reacted by attacking the Diocese.

In 1974, on the feast of [the five hundredth anniversary of the birth of] Bartolomé de Las Casas, the first bishop of this diocese, we organized together with other groups an Indigenous congress [the First Indigenous Congress] which was probably the first of its kind in the history of Chiapas. This Congress was an opportunity for the various Native peoples in the Diocese to come together and become more aware of their identity, unity and strength as Indigenous peoples and communities. The subsequent governments of Chiapas and its power elites have never forgiven us for organizing this congress.

The economic power elites in Chiapas are well connected to those who have political power; that is the way things are all over the world. These people constantly complained about our work to state and federal governments. They even made their voices heard by the Conference of Mexican Bishops, including the Cardinal of Mexico, who they thought was in a position to order us to change our line of pastoral work. They also tried to make contacts with the Vatican asking that I be removed from here. It's a long story!

We learned later that there was an agreement between the Apostolic delegate in Mexico [Gerónimo Prigione], and the Mexican government to get rid of me. My head was offered [by the Apostolic delegate] as a price for re-establishing diplomatic relations between the Mexican state and the Vatican. That is, the Apostolic delegate offered to remove me in return for the Mexican government's agreement to recognize the Mexican Catholic Church and re-establish its diplomatic relations with the Vatican. [This scenario took place during the presidency of Carlos Salinas, 1988-1994]. In order to remove me, they needed some justification. So, they began to accuse me of heterodoxy saying, for example, that my theology was not in accordance with Catholic doctrine, and that I was promoting violence. Obviously, this did not lead anywhere because at the same time the diocese was receiving a broad range of national and international support from many organizations, including yours, Development and Peace. Removing me at that moment would have generated reactions at ecclesial and secular levels, both nationally and internationally. And that is why I am still here.

Since the beginning of 1994, there has been an escalation in the attacks against us. On January 1, 1994, fifteen thousand Indigenous people, according to Mexican Army sources, declared war against this Army. Mexico supposedly was preparing to become part of the first world with the entering into effect of the North American Free Trade Agreement (NAFTA) with Canada and the United States. On that same night, with the declaration of war by the Zapatistas and the situation of poverty in the Indigenous communities which was made known to the world, Mexico appeared to be part of the fourth world. The Mexican government, which has hosted several international meetings on economic development, and which has been marketing its remarkable economic progress to the world, couldn't accept the fact that such a situation existed within its territory. Government officials denied that the causes of the uprising were local. Their propaganda was that the uprising had to have been initiated by foreigners, and that these foreigners included some of the pastoral workers of the diocese of San Cristóbal. Many Mexican government officials insisted on the fact that the Indian peoples were being manipulated by foreigners through a process promoted by our diocesan teams. Their hypothesis has not changed much since. They still believe that we, and the foreign pastoral workers in our diocese, are the cause of the Indian rebellion. They intentionally confuse our support and acknowledgment of the just cause of the rebellion with support of the armed uprising. The government itself agreed with the just cause of the rebellion when it made the Law of Dialogue and Conciliation (Ley Para el Diálogo, la Conciliación y la Paz en Chiapas, 9 de marzo de 1995). That is also what we support, not the armed movement. The last wave of attacks against our diocese are due precisely to this deliberate identification of our diocesan work and support for the just cause of the Indigenous communities with their armed movement.

On January 12, 1994, eleven days after the declaration of war of the EZLN, and under a lot of national and international pressure, the Mexican government offered a cease-fire and the Zapatistas accepted immediately. Three persons were asked to be mediators: myself; Rigoberta Menchu, who did not accept the invitation because, she said, she was not Mexican; and a journalist, who also declined because, he said, he could not maintain the neutrality required for such a task due to the nature of his work. So, I stayed alone in the mediation commission--a one person commission. The government was forced to accept the mediation of the diocese because it was under a lot of pressure from Mexican civil society and from the Indigenous communities.

The government had no desire for peace. It used the discussion table, at which we were present as mediators, to put pressure on the Zapatistas and reduce their political power. There was no genuine pursuit of peace. All through the negotiations, the government continued to attack the diocese of San Cristóbal and the CONAI. Under pressure from the big landowners and their supporters, the Vatican also intervened and an adjunct bishop was named to the diocese. Shortly after arriving in San Cristóbal, Raul Vera, the new bishop, who already knew the diocese, began to see things in the same way we did. He is not opposed to our pastoral process; on the contrary, in him we have another bishop who supports our work.

Recently, the situation with the Vatican has changed. The current Papal Nuncio visited us and we believe that he has a better understanding of our situation. He visited all three dioceses of Chiapas and has clearly demonstrated support to us, and has made recommendations in support of our work. He said things about me that I cannot say about him: he said that he would burn his hands in fire for the bishop of San Cristóbal. He is extremely firm and supportive of our work. This is a big change from the past.

With the government, the situation has not changed much. On three different occasions during his recent visit to Chiapas, the President of the Republic [Ernesto Zedillo] spoke against us accusing us of being promoters of violence. We did not have to answer him this time because many people from his own party criticized his position. But we are now expecting a change--not a radical one, but hopefully an improvement--in our relations with the government, since we decided to dissolve the CONAI. I think our decision was a bit of a shock to the government and it was difficult for them to understand it. One week after it was announced, the government was still attacking the CONAI as if it still existed. The dissolution of the CONAI made it clear to public opinion that the government is not really willing to have direct talks with the Zapatistas--[which was the raison d'être of the CONAI.] They have no intention of fulfilling the agreements reached at San Andrés and the CONAI was used as a scapegoat for their lack of political will.

Are you getting approval and support for your work beyond the Mexican Church? For example, from other churches in the world and the Holy See?

Don Samuel: Do not take my response as being aggressive--that is not the intention. But, when someone asks me this question, I usually respond with another question. Does one need permission to breathe? Do I need permission from you to do good works? That is to say, do we always need to seek approval from the Vatican for whatever we need to do? Not having a direct support or permission, does not mean that what we are doing is wrong!

On January 2, 1994 the three bishops of Chiapas issued a document explaining to the Mexican community what was happening in Chiapas, and we made an ethical judgment on the armed uprising. We stated clearly that we were not in agreement with the armed movement, but that we agreed with the cause of the movement. Since the beginning of the conflict, the Mexican Bishops' Conference has appointed a commission to accompany in solidarity the peace process in Chiapas. The commission has visited Chiapas seven times already; their last visit took place last week and we informed them about the current pastoral action of the diocese.

The Mexican Bishops' Conference has issued several statements since the beginning of the conflict in support of our work and the peace process in Chiapas. The documents they have produced (which we have here) are by now almost the size of a book. The Pope is also well informed about Chiapas--more so now than before--and he has discussed the situation in Chiapas on several occasions with visiting Mexican bishops. But, as in a choir, there are always one or two voices that are out of tune with the rest of the group. This also happens with a Bishops' Conference: there are from time to time one or two voices that are not in full agreement with the rest, and they criticize us.

Can you speak to us about the decision to dissolve the National Mediation Commission (CONAI)? And how do you see the future of the peace process and the role of the diocese in it?

Gonzalo Ituarte: Don Samuel announced the dissolution of the CONAI [on June 7, 1998] because it was the right moment to conclude its work. The decision was made several months after realizing that the CONAI had become useless, because the government did not have the will to negotiate peace. The government does not want war, but it does not want peace either--and it feels comfortable with this situation. The government does not want a military confrontation, because this would be politically and economically harmful to Mexico, and it is not eager to achieve peace because they have the Zapatistas under control through the militarization and paramilitarization of Chiapas. Even if the situation stays like this for years, it does not matter much to the government.

Don Samuel did not resign from the CONAI; the CONAI was dissolved. It has fulfilled its role and its dissolution allows us now as a diocese, and particularly Don Samuel, to step forward in the peace process and be free again to speak. We were bound in a certain way by the structure of the CONAI. As mediators with other members of civil society, and within the legal framework of the negotiation procedures, we were not always free to move as we wished in the process of building peace. So, we had to get rid of this structure so that we could step forward and look for new ways in line with our long tradition of struggle for peace; we have been struggling for peace here in Chiapas for the last forty years. Violence and war have been a permanent situation here.

We have to rethink the way of our participation in the peace process. We are trying to strengthen our presence in the midst of the people and we are searching for new ways of building peace and attending to the real causes of the conflict. For example, at this moment, we are trying to strengthen the reconciliation process within the communities because one key aspect of this conflict has been the internal divisions in the communities. The low intensity war implemented by the government, created confrontations within the communities. Instead of dealing with the real historical and structural causes of the conflict, the government uses these confrontations to try to demonstrate to public opinion that the problem of Chiapas lies within the communities. So, the government created and stimulated confrontations among communities and their organizations, and publicized this in the mass media to fog over the real situation. It is important for us now as a diocese to maintain a presence in the communities, to be a stimulus for reconciliation, and also to be the conscience of the nation by telling the truth about what is really happening in Chiapas.

Mexico has been suffering from a low intensity democracy for the last seventy years. The system is using the low intensity war to stop the pressure for transition to democracy. In this new phase of the peace process, we have to discover the place of the church and the ways in which we can participate. We will continue to work for peace in new ways and we will not resign from our commitment to the cause of the poor and the cause of the Indian peoples. However, we continue to disagree with the use of violence to achieve change. The desperate people here were pushed by the system to violence; they are not violent people by nature.

How can the international community help in this new stage and what can we do in Canada to support your work for peace?

Gonzalo Ituarte: First of all, by fidelity to your own identity. The nature and work of Development and Peace as an organization is very important, in terms of your solidarity with Chiapas. Keeping your people aware of what is happening here, and putting some light pressure on your government from time to time might be helpful. We have had good relations with the Canadian Embassy here in Mexico, and with the various Canadian governments so far. I was recently invited to Canada, along with other people from Mexico, for a reality check with some Canadian officials. The people we met from the Canadian government [in Ottawa] were concerned about the positions of the Mexican government in relation to Chiapas. I think that the relationship of the Canadian government with the Indigenous people in your own country, is an important experience from which many countries in Latin America could learn something. You have developed a new approach with the Native peoples and this could stimulate here an interest in the Canadian experience. Canada is an example to the Mexican government to not be afraid of the Indian peoples' demands for autonomy because it is happening there and it is working.

There is an interest in Chiapas among the international community. The Mexican government is putting up many obstacles to prevent people from coming and staying here. I was talking to a Canadian woman yesterday here in San Cristóbal who wanted to stay here for two months, and she was given a visa for only ten days. That should be unacceptable to you. You should demand to be treated as human beings in Mexico with the right to come, visit, make friends, and learn about the lives of other people. It is very important for us to see people like you come here and support small groups freely and without harassment. You probably came with tourist visas to visit us as friends and to see the Mayan ruins--or better, the ruined Mayas. Bringing the reality of what you see here to the consciousness of the Canadian people, and your government, is important. It is not possible to do business with a country that treats you as dangerous foreigners and treats the Mexicans you visit here as enemies of the state.

Our government is hiding behind a barricade and does not want to show its true face and accept a transition to democracy. It wants to hide the problems we have with the Indigenous people and make us look as if we are similar to you, so that you will feel comfortable here. One thing to know is that the Mexican government, especially the president and his friends, think in English. That is a great danger to Mexico. We do not want to become Canadians or gringos. We want to be Mexican and live with you as different peoples respecting each other. The government of Mexico tries to make us very similar to our neighbours in the North. We do not want you to find people similar to you in Mexico, we want Canadians to visit Mexico and find Mexicans, and celebrate what we are together.

How is the 'option for the poor' being lived today here in the diocese of San Cristóbal?

Don Samuel: All the work that has been done here, and I believe it is the same in other places in Latin America, can be summarized by saying that it is helping the Indigenous people who have taken steps to become *subjects* of their own history. More than helping by offering things to them, what is needed is to offer them the space to express themselves as subjects of their own history and not to deny them this historic opportunity. This was emphasized by the Pope when he came to Yucatan in August of 1993, a few months before the Indigenous uprising. John Paul II said then to the Indigenous people of the continent, who came to meet him in Izamal, Yucatan, "You are the subjects of the new evangelization, and subjects of the integral transformation of the continent."

When the Pope was in Santo Domingo in 1992, he was not feeling well and was tired. He promised the Indigenous people present there that he would come back to visit them. So he came to Yucatan shortly afterwards and said these two things which are very significant, even shocking. The Indigenous peoples of the continent, said the Pope, are the subject of evangelization. Everybody knows perhaps, that people evangelize other people who are like them: workers evangelize workers, and campesinos evangelize campesinos. But to say that the Indian peoples are the subject of the evangelization of all the continent, was really significant. The Pope was very clear about that. What do we see in this affirmation? The Indian people are oppressed all over the continent. We cannot deny the efforts of people such as Rigoberta Menchu in this regard--giving her the Nobel Prize was a recognition of the urgency of the situation of the Indigenous peoples in Latin America. The other affirmation made by the Pope was that the Indigenous peoples are the subject of the integral transformation of the system in Latin America.

I am sometimes criticized for promoting autochthonous Indian churches. Some believe that this will separate the Indian communities from the rest of the church, and will not allow them to participate in the liberation process with the rest of society. My argument is that they will be an active force of change and liberation, only when they experience this liberation together as a people. The Indian people are oppressed not only politically and economically, but also culturally. They are emerging and joining other culturally oppressed groups such as Women, Asian and Black peoples as protagonists of transformation. The Indian uprising is not only happening in Chiapas and for Chiapas, it is happening all over the world, and reaching far beyond Chiapas. The proof of this is that people like yourselves, and many others from Europe, are coming here to Chiapas to see what is happening. People from Europe are saying, that the struggle of the Indian people here is bringing them a message of hope for the future.

The cultural struggle of the Indian people, is important for the transformation of the global system.

Jorge Santiago: I would like to make reference to some important historical events, in relation to the option for the poor in this diocese. After Don Samuel came to Chiapas in 1960, the Apostolic delegate offered his support to the diocese and helped to found two centres for the formation of catechists in San Cristóbal: one for women administered by the Sisters of the Divine Pastor, and another for men administered by the Marist Brothers (the latter was later moved to Comitán). This project was begun in 1963-4 and it continues today. Many people were formed in these centres: there are around 8,000 active catechists in the diocese today who were trained there. The formation sessions usually last from two to three months, and some last for a whole year.

Don Samuel also founded mission centres: the Jesuit mission in the Bachajón area, the mission of the Dominicans in the Ocosingo region, and of the Missionaries of the Sacred Heart of Jesus and Mary in Tenejapa (which included the parishes of Oxchuc and Huistan). The vision of these important centres was to create conditions for pastoral work with and inside the communities, and not along the lines of centralized traditional parish work. The missionaries began to study the languages and the culture of the Indigenous communities; the efforts of the Jesuits were significant in this regard. A new vision and concept of missionary work which included economic development also began to emerge. The diocesan pastoral work was transformed by creating new pastoral zones and teams with a common vision. This model of organization continues to the present day. These were the developments which took place in the mid 1960s.

Then came the Second Latin American Bishops' Conference (CELAM II) in Medellín in 1968, at which Don Samuel participated and presented a paper on Evangelization in Latin America. Since that time, the diocese has been playing an important role at the continental level in the areas of evangelization, culture, and social development;

our pastoral work was not done in isolation, but rather we were part of a broader process all over Latin America. Since that time also, an important link between the work that Don Samuel does as bishop of San Cristóbal, his work at the Department of Missions of CELAM in the areas of pastoral work with the Indigenous peoples, and the development of an Indian theology was established. Here in the diocese, we are living these developments in a very concrete way; in a way, our diocese has been a laboratory for testing these developments.

Another important date was 1975. That was the date of the first diocesan assembly, shortly after the First Indigenous Congress of 1974. This assembly was held to respond to the proposals that came out from the Congress. The Indigenous communities wanted to construct their projects themselves, and not have them imposed from the outside. The question we were asking ourselves as a diocese then was how to support the work that was being born in the communities. The idea of holding regular diocesan assemblies to promote this process emerged during that time and it continues today.

The last very important date is 1999, that is when we will be doing an evaluation and restructuring of our pastoral process based on the experience of the communities--not of the hierarchical structure. This process will mark the end of a four year diocesan synod, and the fortieth year of Don Samuel's time as bishop of the diocese. This will be a moment for us to evaluate our option for the poor and for a new church and society.

Don Samuel: I would like to use this opportunity to thank you for your visit. We are what we are today thanks to the support of groups like you. Thank you for these many years of companionship. I was invited to Canada by Development and Peace more than once and I have also visited some Native communities in your country.